Healthy Mindsets for
Little Kids

by the same author

Healthy Mindsets for Super Kids
A Resilience Programme for Children Aged 7–14
Stephanie Azri
Illustrated by Sid Azri
ISBN 978 1 84905 315 0
eISBN 978 0 85700 698 1

of related interest

Helping Children to Build Self-Esteem
A Photocopiable Activities Book
Deborah Plummer
Illustrated by Alice Harper
ISBN 978 1 84310 488 9
eISBN 978 1 84642 609 4

Being Me (and Loving It)
Stories and activities to help build self-esteem, confidence,
positive body image and resilience in children
Naomi Richards and Julia Hague
ISBN 978 1 84905 713 4
eISBN 978 1 78450 236 2

Positive Body Image for Kids
A Strengths-Based Curriculum for Children Aged 7–11
Ruth MacConville
ISBN 978 1 84905 539 0
eISBN 978 1 78450 047 4

No More Stinking Thinking
A workbook for teaching children positive thinking
Joann Altiero
ISBN 978 1 84310 839 9
eISBN 978 1 84642 579 0

Healthy Mindsets for
Little Kids

A Resilience Programme to Help Children Aged 5–9
with Anger, Anxiety, Attachment, Body Image,
Conflict, Discipline, Empathy and Self-Esteem

Dr Stephanie Azri

Illustrated by Sid Azri
Consultant: Claire Kelly

Jessica Kingsley *Publishers*
London and Philadelphia

First published in 2020
by Jessica Kingsley Publishers
73 Collier Street
London N1 9BE, UK
and
400 Market Street, Suite 400
Philadelphia, PA 19106, USA

www.jkp.com

Copyright © Stephanie Azri 2020
Illustrations copyright © Sid Azri 2020
Foreword copyright © Raymond Ho 2020
Consultant: Claire Kelly

Front cover illustrations by Sid Azri.

Library of Congress Cataloging in Publication Data
A CIP catalog record for this book is available from the Library of Congress

British Library Cataloguing in Publication Data
A CIP catalogue record for this book is available from the British Library

ISBN 978 1 78592 865 9
eISBN 978 1 78592 869 7

Printed and bound by CPI Group (UK) Ltd, Croydon, CR0 4YY

Contents

Foreword

Having known Dr Azri for a few years, I have seen her to be an incredibly passionate and experienced clinical social worker with extensive experience in working with families struggling with severe mental health difficulties. I am particularly impressed with her ability to translate sophisticated clinical concepts and theories into practical strategies and skills that are easy to learn and understand. When Dr Azri informed me that she was writing a programme to help young children develop resilience, I was expecting a child-friendly programme teaching many foundational skills to develop such resilience.

Resilience entails people's ability to withstand and rebound from adverse life events and challenges. Children who are resilient are more likely to become adults who possess the strengths and resources that enable them to respond appropriately to stressful crises and adversities. They develop the abilities to 'struggle well' over time and heal from difficult and/or painful life events, moving on to live fully rather than being blocked from growth or trapped or victimised. Assisting children and young people to develop resilience has been a goal of the utmost importance for child and youth mental health professionals and scholars for many years.

Having worked in the child and youth mental health field for the last 20 years, I have gained an understanding of exactly how important it is for young children to learn these skills and have seen first-hand the consequences of failing to acquire these essential building blocks for developing resilience. While there are many good early intervention programmes like Incredible Years, Mind Matters, Aussie Optimism, Friends etc., a large majority of these programmes are targeted at teenagers and require extensive training for professionals to be able to deliver them. *Healthy Mindset for Little Kids* is unique as it is designed to make resilience skills and training accessible to as many children as possible, with a focus on children aged 5–9 years old.

When you start reading this book, you will notice that this actually holds more resemblance to an easy-to-follow programme manual than anything else. It provides you with practical steps to deliver 10 skill-based training sessions to young children and their families. Each session has tips for facilitators, skill developing activities, child-friendly materials and tools to help engage and guide parents to reinforce their children's skill development. Furthermore, the programme design integrates the concepts of attachment, family relationship and child development as the fundamental context for skill building in young children. Following the sequence of the programme, you will start learning about a child's primary attachment environment. Then you will be introduced to skills and activities that assist children to lay the foundation to develop the concept of self, self-confidence and positive thinking. You will then move on to skills that assist children to manage self and interpersonal relationships, and finally the affect and emotional regulation skills that are essential for children to develop in preparation for the teenage years. These are essential building blocks for developing skills in resilience.

If you are interested in an easy-to-follow how-to programme manual to assist you to deliver a resilience building programme, Dr Azri's book *Healthy Mindset for Little Kids* is an essential and highly effective tool which I would very highly recommend.

Raymond Ho
Deputy Director
Child and Youth Academic Clinical Unit
Metro South Addiction and Mental Health Services
Metro South Hospital and Health Services – Queensland Health

Acknowledgements

First of all, I'd like to tell a short story about how the very first idea of a programme for young children came about. Four years ago, an amazing family consultant and friend of mine, Claire Kelly from Communication Kinnections (www.communicationkinnections.com) facilitated the *Healthy Mindsets for Super Kids* programme and her insights incredibly strengthened my work. She and I came up with an idea for a programme for preschool kids, and while the idea wasn't able to be pursued for various reasons and was quite different from this new product, Claire was the first person who believed that a version for the younger age group had value and for this, I am very grateful.

A huge thank you to the Metro South Mental Health Services Logan recovery team (QLD Health) for motivating me. Thank you Peter, Emma, Amanda and Iris for the support, the follow ups and believing in the Healthy Mindsets programmes. You were the highlight of my year. Watching my small contribution grow and provide amazing support to our local families has humbled me beyond words. Without you, it could never have happened and I will be forever thankful.

Of course, thank you to Jessica Kingsley Publishers and the whole team. Especially, my editor, Andrew, for his amazing and efficient advice and support in this process. I'm excited to be working on the adult version with JKP next.

Most importantly, thank you to the wonderful families, children and their parents for their participation and willingness to join in this fun venture. It is such a privilege, one that is unique, special and amazing. I can't wait to see where this goes!

Please join me on my Facebook page at www.facebook.com/StephanieAzriAuthor or join my mailing list at www.stephanieazri.com for free updates and resources. Please, please, please, don't hesitate to let me know about your own work with the programme. I'd genuinely love to hear from you.

Yours in resilience,
Stephanie

Introduction

The notion of resilience has emerged as an important factor influencing children's responses to adverse events and in the last 15 years resilience theory and resilience programmes for children have flourished globally. While the concept started with the investigation of resilience of children of mentally ill parents, it continued with other at-risk groups such as children from low socioeconomic backgrounds and those with learning difficulties.[1] The study of resilience quickly led to a shift towards strength-based models which would apply to all groups of children. In essence, resilience provides a framework for understanding the ways and the reasons why children respond differently to difficult events. The definition of resilience has remained clear: resilience is one's ability to overcome negative events.

To me, as a clinical social worker and as a mother, resilience should be afforded to all children and their families. The concept that resilience should be regarded as a preventative notion, teaching fundamental building blocks of skills in a systematic way to all children in routine settings, stands out to me as a basic right for all kids with the potential to drastically improve their lives. Communication skills, emotional regulation, grief and loss, positive thinking, social skills and self-esteem are commonly taught in clusters throughout schools and counselling groups; a preventative programme encompassing all of those skills emerged as a potential solution for older children and 5 years ago, *Healthy Mindsets for Super Kids* came to life after I'd struggled to find an acccessible and affordable resilience programme for my own children. What I didn't expect was how fast and widespread the programme would grow. To watch this programme get taught in local schools, counselling centres and community organisations over the world has been humbling and huge motivation to consider new ways to make it even more accessible – the goal being that every child gets the opportunity to learn resilience and life skills routinely.

This year, the programme was adopted by QLD Health and facilitated by a team of amazing and dedicated staff. Watching their enthusiasm and expertise while running groups for children and sessions for facilitators, as well as their feedback on gaps for the younger age groups, gave me the spark I needed to design *Healthy Mindsets for Little Kids*. The feedback we received over the last couple of years was that a programme for the younger age group was needed and would make a vital contribution to this field of practice and so, with great pride, I present this new book to you today. *Healthy Mindsets for Little Kids*

---

1   Werner, K. (1993) 'Risk, resilience and recover: Perspectives from the Kauai longitudinal study.' *Development and Psychopathology 5*, 503–515.

is a resilience programme for children from 5–9 years old. It is designed for the kids who are that little bit too young to participate in the older programme and who could benefit from extra parental engagement. All sessions are fun, interactive and designed to be non-threatening. They include heavy parent/carer involvement and are designed to look at the child in a family unit, rather than on their own.

As in the previous book, this new programme is built over ten sessions:

1. Identity and attachment

2. Self-esteem and confidence

3. Self soothing and emotional regulation

4. Positive thinking

5. Communication and body language

6. Social skills

7. Learning about discipline

8. Anger management

9. Anxiety management

10. Healthy minds and healthy bodies.

Each module contains a lesson plan, discussion topics, exercises, games and activities as well as some worksheets. In addition, each module is illustrated by a friendly animal character representing that particular skill. Finally, each module ends on a practical activity to reinforce the skill taught as well as a parent challenge sheet. The modules can be used all together or individually, and in a group setting or in a private session. Appendices are included at the end of the book for professionals wishing to run the programme in their practice, groups or organisations, and please always feel free to contact me for advice, input or feedback. This imaginative resource is a complete programme ideal for teachers, early childhood educators, GPs, psychologists, occupational therapists (OTs), nurses, therapists, social workers and family support workers working or wanting to work on resilience building with children and their families.

For more information and tips on building resilience in families, visit my website at www.stephanieazri.com and join the mailing list.

Session | 1

Identity and Attachment Module

1. Welcome and introductions

The warm and non-threatening introduction of the participants amongst themselves is vital for the group to start forming in a positive way. Many of the children who will be involved in the programme will be children who have attachment, social or communication issues. Some of the parents who will be involved may feel vulnerable, perhaps burnt out or hesitant to discuss their parenting in a group setting. Ensuring that the introduction goes smoothly will facilitate the nurturing of all children and carers and help them to feel valued in the group. Before starting the session, ensure that participants are aware of exit points and location of toilets. Give particular instructions relevant to your group. The facilitator will introduce him or herself and allow every child to introduce themselves to the rest of the group.

> 'Hi everyone, welcome to *Healthy Mindsets for Little Kids*, a fun programme designed to teach us to create positive thoughts and to use them to make us happy and healthy. Let's just start with introducing ourselves to the group. We'll go around in a circle and I'll start. My name is _____ and I am going to be your "teacher" for *Healthy Mindsets for Little Kids*.'

> ✓ Housekeeping (toilets and rules)
>
> ✓ Purpose of programme; group rules
>
> ✓ Introducing our names to the group.

2. Introductory activity

Sitting down as a group in a circle, spread Strength cards (or similar product) on the ground and allow each child and carer to choose a card that represents something they enjoy. This holds a double purpose: to work as an icebreaker and to provide all children and carers the opportunity to talk about themselves and one of their hobbies/strengths/skills. The facilitator should assist them in taking turns and sharing the reason they chose any particular card.

> 'Thank you all for this. I look forward to getting to know you, and to do that today we're going to do an activity. Today's session is on getting to know each other and to start looking at ourselves in a good and healthy way. I'm going to spread some cards on the floor and when I'm done I'm going to ask all of you to take one card that you think represents something you like or are good at.'

✓ Thank children and carers for participating

✓ Reinforce purpose of session today (identity and attachment)

✓ Strength card activity (to pick something the children are good at or enjoy and share it as a group).

---

3. Who are we? We are all special

In this section, the facilitator will discuss a little bit about the likes/dislikes the participants have identified in themselves. He/she will explain that we are all different and unique, and that makes us all very special. The facilitator will comment on a positive unique feature for each child, emphasising their uniqueness (pointing out their beautiful curls, warm smile, lovely manners etc.).

'We are all different and special. Some of us have brown hair, others blue eyes, some live with their parents, carers, and some have lots of brothers and sisters while some of us don't. We all belong to someone who loves us very much, even if it's different for everyone.'

DISCUSSION

Children are all special, though may look different, have different lives and families, things they like and don't like or little things that make them 'them'.

Could you turn to your mum, dad or carer, and look at the things that are the same between you, and the things that are different (hair, eyes, body shape, smile, likes and dislikes).

What do you notice?

✓ Who are we? We're all different, yet unique

✓ Even with our mum, dad or carer, there are things that are the same and things that are different

✓ Come back as a group and share.

4. Who am I?

The facilitator will thank all participants for sharing their thoughts and experiences. The first worksheet of the identity and attachment module will be presented. This worksheet contains the 'All about me' exercise. As with all worksheets, carers will be responsible to ensure that children of all literacy and attention levels are assisted with completing it. The exercise involves children drawing themselves with the help of their carers, other children or the facilitator, with the purpose of discovering and discussing their 'unique' identity.

Group members are encouraged to consider their traits both from a physical and personality point of view, as well as the things they enjoy doing, as they explore their own identity. Facilitators are encouraged to invite a discussion with the group regarding the things that make them special and unique, in order to signal or provide a cue for the group members regarding the expectation of the activity. This broader group discussion will enable the participants to understand the expectation of the activity.

WORKSHEET 1: ALL ABOUT ME

Each participant should be provided with a worksheet and should be encouraged to commence colouring in the figure, including adding the features of the face to reflect their mood or personality. Once each member of the group is settled with the worksheet and has a range of resources to colour in the figure, facilitators are encouraged to move around the room discussing with each participant the things they like about themselves, their 'favourite person in the world', their 'best friend' and the things they like to do. The responses to these questions should be documented by the children and/or their carers on the worksheet and participants should be encouraged to say aloud the statements documented on their worksheets. Group participants may require assistance or prompting with their responses.

Group participants should be encouraged to bring back their worksheets to the whole group and an invitation to discuss thoughts should be facilitated. The aim is to have all children identify their uniqueness and feel good about who they are.

DISCUSSION

Would you like to tell us about your picture? Have you learnt anything about you? What makes you very special? What about other people? How are they special too?

- ✓ Worksheet 1: 'All about me'

- ✓ Children to draw themselves while learning to identify uniqueness in themselves and others

- ✓ Come back as a group and share.

Closing activity: Me and my family

The facilitator will engage the children around their family units. The purpose of this section is to demonstrate to the children they are loved and belong to a family, even if they may look different from one another. It is important to stress that contemporary families come in many shapes and sizes and facilitators are encouraged to celebrate diversity and difference. This activity has the potential to identify children within the group as 'different' to the norm and, as such, facilitators are encouraged to be vigilant to ensure every child feels included and supported.

'We are all different and our families come in many shapes and sizes. Some of us may live with our parents, others may live with a grandparent or a relative...and some of us may live in two houses with step mums or dads – this is okay. During this activity we will get a chance to see who is in the family of other children in the group and get an understanding of who is important to them. It is very important we don't judge others or make negative comments when someone's family is different to our own. This activity is about each of us having fun and sharing our experiences.'

RESOURCES NEEDED

- Large sheets of cardboard

- Pencils, crayons, felt pens etc.

- Worksheet 2 template (will need multiple copies)

- Scissors

- Glue

- Craft resources, such as stickers, glitter etc. for decoration.

Using the template provided in this module cut out the bodies on firm paper or cardboard for children to identify who they consider to be 'in their family'. Children are encouraged to identify whom they are acknowledging as a family member by using craft resources, e.g. crayons, colouring in pencils etc., identifying the individuals' favourite colour, their regular clothing and any distinguishing features of the person. The names of the individuals the child is identifying should also be recorded on the template. Faces have been deliberately left out of the templates and children should be encouraged to draw the faces for each of their family members, reflecting their personality and the disposition of the person they have identified.

'I'd like us to create our families now. You can pick a little person for each member of your family and glue them to the big piece of cardboard. Then I'd like you to write the name of the person at the top and draw them. You can use the decorations on the table to make your family any way you choose. It's important to see that families come in different shapes and sizes and they're all great.'

✓ Worksheet 2 'All about my family'

✓ Recognising the similarities and differences in other people's families

✓ Understanding who is the child's primary attachment and any complexities in the child's family unit.

Closing down the session

Children and facilitators should come together at the conclusion of the session to discuss the learning outcomes. Children are encouraged to consider today's activities and their future 'fun' involvement in the programme. Some of these include:

- The rules (either group or individual), i.e. how to behave etc.

- Highlighting the identity and attachment activities 'All about me' and 'All about my family' – children should be encouraged to say out loud the things they have identified throughout the session to reinforce the activity.

- Identification of the most significant people in the child's life, enabling the child to verbalise to the facilitator who they consider to be in their family.

- It is vital to ensure that all children and their carers leave feeling supported and empowered.

- Remind parents to help their children prepare one show and tell for next week (one that represents a strength or something unique about them) and to bring one white t-shirt for the next module's activity.

KATIE THE KANGAROO LOVES WARM CUDDLES

SESSION 1: PARENTS' CORNER

'I AM LOVED!'

Today we discussed our identities and families, and the children should have identified what makes them special, even when they are different. What we know is that accepting who we are and feeling a sense of belonging fosters good positive minds and attachment, so it's important to build on it.

This week, in addition to getting you to discuss your child's special traits and loving family members with them, I'd like to challenge you with some exercises to reflect on attachment in general.

✓ Can you identify your own attachment with others? Who were the important people in your life growing up? How important were they?

✓ Can you think of any ways your child could be supported with the unique attributes they share?

✓ What kind of quality time with your child's important people could you facilitate, promote or organise?

✓ Physical touch and kind words are often positive ways for children to feel special and attach to caregivers. Have you told your kids you love them today? Given them a hug or laughed with them?

WORKSHEET 1: All about me

My name is: _____

I am _____ years of age

My birthday is: _____

I am _____ cm tall

Today's date is: _____

MY BEST FRIEND IS

_____

MY FAVOURITE PERSON IN THE WORLD IS

_____

_____

_____

I LIKE TO

_____

_____

_____

_____

_____

_____

_____

WORKSHEET 2: All about my family

This template should be copied so that children can use one for each member of their immediate family. Each template should then be glued to a large piece of cardboard for ease of decorating.

Session | 2

Self-Esteem and Confidence Module

1. Welcoming participants

The facilitator will welcome the children and their parents back for their second session and ensure that all children have brought something for their 'show and tell'. The item or presentation should highlight a strength of the child, and parents are welcome to participate. Today, some of the children will be very excited to return while others may continue to feel uncomfortable, especially if the group members did not know each other prior to the beginning of the programme. The facilitator should take a few minutes to reintroduce everyone's names and facilitate friendship groups. A brief summary of last week's session will occur. The facilitator should ensure all children have an equal opportunity to voice their thoughts in the group.

> 'Hi everyone, welcome back to *Healthy Mindsets for Little Kids*. I'd like to take a minute to go around the circle and ask everyone what they thought of last week's session. What do you remember about what we learnt?'

✓ Housekeeping refresher (toilets, rules and names)

✓ Purpose of session today

✓ Remind the group of everyone's names

✓ Thank participants for feedback about last week.

---

2. Introductory activity

Sitting down as a group in a circle, spread Strength cards (or similar product) on the ground and allow each child and each parent to choose a card that represents something they are proficient at. This holds a double purpose: to work as an icebreaker and to provide all children with the opportunity to talk about themselves and one of their strengths. The facilitator should assist them in taking turns and sharing the reason they chose any particular card.

> 'Thank you all for this. I look forward to having fun with you, and to do that today we're going to do an activity. Today's session is on getting to know each other and to start looking at ourselves in a good and happy way. I'm going to spread some cards on the floor and when I'm done I'm going to ask all of you to take one card that shows something you are good at.'

✓ Thank children for participating

✓ Reinforce purpose of session today (self-esteem and confidence)

✓ Strength card activity (to pick something the children are good at and share it as a group).

3. Who are we? We all have positive and negatives

In this section, the facilitator will discuss the strengths the participants have identified in themselves. Positive reinforcement and encouragement should occur and small things should be celebrated too! The facilitator will explain that we are all different: good at some things, and not so good at other things, emphasising that this is normal. The facilitator will continue by discussing how the children may feel when they struggle at doing something, but that the important thing is to keep trying (sports, kindy, home activities etc.).

'We are all different and so sometimes we might find we struggle at some things others are really good at. What we need to remember is that the important thing is to do our best and to keep trying! Sometimes though when we're around people who are good at things we may feel a little sad or frustrated and we may even forget that we're good at different things.'

DISCUSSION
Has that happened to you? Have you ever felt frustrated, sad or angry because you struggled at doing something? Talk to your mum or dad, or a friend next to you, and tell us a story about feeling really good about something you could do by yourself, or wishing you could do something you're having trouble with.

✓ Who are we? We're all different and have positives and negatives.

✓ It's normal to feel frustrated when we can't do something, but the important thing is to try our best and to focus on something that we are good at.

✓ Get in a pair and discuss our experiences. Come back as a group and share.

4. Show and tell activity

ACTIVITY 1

The facilitator will thank all participants for sharing their thoughts and experiences. The first activity of the self-esteem module will be presented. This activity should have been planned before this week, and all children/parents advised at the end of the last session. This activity focuses on children presenting a skill or an item that represents something they are good at (it could be playing a short piece on the violin; it could be a soccer trophy or represent a day when the child did something really positive. It could focus on any area (e.g. academic, sports, social, spiritual, family etc.). The purpose of this activity is to explore all of those areas and identify things in areas the children may actually enjoy or be good at. Additionally, the purpose of this activity is to identify that we may not be good in all areas and that this is okay, as well as teaching children to encourage success in their peers and be happy for them.

'Now that we've started talking about how we feel about being good and bad at different things, we're going to play a game. Who has heard of "show and tell"? We are going to take turns, and show our group something that we are really good at or loved doing. We can ask our mum or dad for help too. Who would like to start?'

✓ Activity 1: Show and tell

✓ Practise listening to our friends' strengths while being proud of ours too.

DISCUSSION

How did it feel to show our friends something we loved doing and were good at?
How did it feel to watch and encourage our friends too?
Come back as a group and share.

Closing down the session

The facilitator will summarise the lesson and activity with the participants, building on what they shared and expressed.

'Being comfortable with the things we're good at as well as the things we're not so good at is what gives us good self-esteem. Self-esteem helps us be happy and achieve heaps in our lives. If you remember your good points and focus on them rather than the negatives, you will grow more self-esteem.'

> ✓ Self-esteem is important. Accepting our challenges while focusing on positives will help us be happy.

Closing activity: Positive self-view shirts

Participants will be making 'positive self-view shirts' to remind themselves of their strengths and the fact that having weaknesses does not make them 'faulty'.

This activity will allow the participants to design shirts which they will wear, symbolising their strengths, positive self-esteem as well as what they have learnt during the lesson. The facilitator will distribute one shirt per child (or may have requested the children to bring their own). Participants are to place one layer of paper between the two layers of the shirt (as ink may go through). Children will think of symbols, pictures or words, which remind them of their strengths and positive identity. The facilitator will walk amongst the children, prompting them if required, and sharing ideas with each individual child of their strengths based on the discussions that have taken place today and worksheets filled out. The children will spend the next 20 minutes drawing this on their shirts with the markers. Words, pictures, symbols may be used and 'freestyle' art will be encouraged. The shirts should look uplifting, positive and be unique to each child. The facilitator will praise participants for their efforts and results.

RESOURCES NEEDED

- White shirts
- Fabric markers
- Newspaper to place between layers of material (shirts).

ANNIE THE ANT IS SMALL BUT STRONG! JUST LIKE YOU!

|

SESSION 2: PARENTS' CORNER

'I AM SPECIAL!'

Today we discussed our strengths and weaknesses, and the children should have identified the benefits of supporting their friends through their own strengths and weaknesses. What we know is that accepting who we are and feeling a sense of pride fosters good positive minds and self-worth, so it's important to build on it.

This week, in addition to getting you to discuss your child's strengths, team spirit and efforts in trying new things with them, I'd like to challenge you with some exercises to reflect on self-esteem in general.

✓ Can you identify your own strengths and weaknesses? How do you feel about them?

✓ Can you think of ways your child could be influenced to have good self-esteem in their home life?

✓ What kind of comments might you (or someone else) make around your child that could be tweaked to foster positive self-esteem? (It's human nature to be unhappy about ourselves.) This is really about self-awareness.

✓ What kind of praise and support could you facilitate or promote with your child on a regular basis?

Session | 3

Self Soothing and Emotional Regulation Module

1. Welcome participants

Generally, by the third session, the children have begun to form friendships and are less anxious about the setting. Parents and carers are generally also more relaxed and it is not unusual for children and parents to mingle in their own groups a bit more. Friendships should be encouraged; however, parent–child partnerships should continue to occur during the formal part of the sessions.

'Hi boys and girls, and parents. It's lovely to have you back. This week we are going to talk about our feelings. Who knows what feelings are? Feelings can make us feel good, sometimes sad, or really happy. Have you felt good feelings before? What about other types of feelings? Let's play a game to discover more about feelings.'

2. Introductory activity

Sitting down as a group in a circle, spread Bear cards (or similar product) on the ground and allow each child and carer to choose a card that represents a facial expression of their choice. This holds a double purpose: to work as an icebreaker for the session and to provide all children and carers with the opportunity to talk about feelings and in particular a feeling that they might be experiencing right now. The facilitator should assist them in taking turns and sharing the reason they chose any particular card.

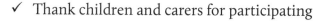

'Thank you all for this. I look forward to hearing all about your feelings, and to do that today we're going to do an activity. Today's session is on getting to understand our feelings and ways to share our feelings in a nice and healthy way. Look at all the faces. Do you know how they're all different? Some are happy, some are sad. Some seem shy and others a little mad. So, I'm going to spread some cards on the floor and when I'm done I'm going to ask all of you to take one card that you think represents how you feel right now.'

✓ Thank children and carers for participating

✓ Reinforce purpose of session today (feelings and emotions management)

✓ Bear card activity (to pick a facial expression that represents how the children are feeling right now, and share it as a group).

---

3. Imagine all the feelings activity

In this section, the facilitator will discuss a little bit about the feelings participants have identified in themselves. He/she will explain that we all can experience different feelings at different times, and that this is normal. The facilitator will comment that there are ways to manage our feelings and that we will learn about some of those tricks today.

Once the children have acknowledged the purpose of today's lesson, the facilitator will utilise the Bear cards from the introductory activity and invite the children to guess what feeling the bears on the cards might feel (other products could be used). Children should be encouraged to participate, invited to guess feelings or what might have happened to the bear to cause that feeling.

'It's normal for us to feel different emotions when things are happening. Imagine how you might feel if you got an award at school? Would you feel happy? Proud? Excited? A little nervous? What about if you had to sing a song in front of the whole class? Nervous? Happy? Angry? Let's play a game with the bears now. Who can tell me what that bear (picking different cards) might feel right now? What might be happening for him/her?'

DISCUSSION

How would you feel if you lost your favourite toy? What about if your mum, dad or carer took you to a theme park tomorrow?
Would these feelings feel different? Do you remember a time where you felt these?

✓ What are feelings?

✓ What happens when we feel happy, sad, angry, excited, scared, proud etc.?

✓ Come back as a group and share.

---

4. *Inside Out* movie activity

The facilitator will thank all participants for sharing their thoughts and experiences. The facilitator will then have prepared a movie section (Disney's *Inside Out* is a great choice, however other options include short snippets of home videos, YouTube clips or other children's films). The facilitator may have prepared a screen, cushions to lean on and perhaps a treat (popcorn is a healthy option). Children and parents should be encouraged to relax and enjoy the clip while trying to pay attention to the emotions of the characters etc. Once the movie part has been watched, the facilitator will settle the participants back ready for discussion. Then, in parent–child pairs, and with the facilitator ensuring the safety of the group, the dyads will discuss the following questions.

> ✓ How did the boy/girl/animal etc. feel in the movie clip? How do you know?
>
> ✓ What made them feel better or could have made them feel better?
>
> ✓ What about you? Tell us about a time where you felt sad/happy/angry/scared/ excited etc. What happened in your body? What did you do? What helped make you feel better?

5. Brainstorming fun

Once the treats and cushions are put away, the facilitator will thank the children and the adults for their participation. Within the large group, the discussion will progress from understanding feelings to naming helpful strategies to regulate emotions. These should be age appropriate, and relevant to the children involved. A whiteboard could be used to record the answers (drawing may be used if children are too young to read).

> **DISCUSSION**
>
> As a large group, let's discuss the things that can help us feel better when we're feeling sad, or angry or frightened. What kind of things may work for you? Did you want to share with the group?

Some of the answers may include:
- Cuddles
- A warm cocoa
- A bubble bath
- Hugging a teddy
- Snuggling on the couch with Mum/Dad/significant other
- Playing a game
- Reading a book
- Playing in the backyard
- A distraction of their choice.

The facilitator should ensure that each child's answer is valued and reinforced, and that all participants feel equally supported in the group. The facilitator should summarise all the answers and praise the children for their ideas. This section will form the basis for the end activity, therefore it is important to summarise as a whole group.

✓ Can feelings sometimes feel good or yucky?

✓ What 'things' can make children feel better?

✓ Come back as a group and share.

Closing activity: Me and my feeling good treasure map

The facilitator will engage the children around their feelings and their identified 'feel good' strategies. The purpose of this section is to demonstrate to the children that all feelings are healthy, and that they have the power to contain feelings and make themselves feel good. Children should be assisted in absorbing their own emotional regulation strategies and invited to consider new ones as well. Parents and children, together, should be discussing ways to implement these at home.

'Today, we've spoken about our feelings and ways we can make these feelings better. Some of our friends gave us new ideas, so with the help of our mum, dad or carer, we might be able to practise them at home this week. To finish today's session, let's do a craft activity about this.'

RESOURCES NEEDED

- Printed coloured A3 paper

- Pencils, crayons, felt pens etc.

- Worksheet 1 template

- Cut outs of emotional regulation strategies

- Glue

- Craft resources such as stickers for decoration.

Using the template provided in this module, the facilitator will have prepared a large piece of paper featuring a happy face and cut out the 'strategies' prior to the children arriving for group. The purpose is for the children to identify and select appropriate emotional regulation strategies to help them regulate and feel happy and settled again. Children will be encouraged to identify strategies they may use or like, and glue them all around the happy face on the large piece of paper. The facilitator is encouraged to go around the tables and provide encouragement and feedback to participants.

'I'd like us to find strategies that may help us feel good and turn our sad or angry emotions into happy ones. On the tables, I have given you a big paper with a happy face, because we love to feel happy, rather than sad! I'd like us to pick activities from the little cut out papers that may make you feel really good. When you have chosen them, you may glue them to your worksheet and colour it in.'

✓ Worksheet 1: 'Me and my feeling good treasure map'

✓ Recognising strategies that may make children feel better

✓ Understanding which strategies may work for each child and getting parents to acknowledge these.

Closing down the session

Children and facilitators should come together at the conclusion of the session to discuss the learning outcomes. Children are encouraged to consider the tasks involved, which include:

✓ Recognising our feelings

✓ Thinking of ways to help ourselves feel better

✓ Getting children and parents to commit to trying these during the week.

ELLIE THE ELEPHANT CAN HANDLE HER FEELINGS LIKE A PRO!

SESSION 3: PARENTS' CORNER

'ALL ABOUT MY FEELINGS'

Today we discussed our feelings and ways to make these feel nice. The children should have identified ways to regulate their emotions in ways that are age- and developmentally appropriate and safe. I would like to encourage you to help them with this task this week. It is normal for young children to struggle, even not to master the strategies at all. This module is about planting a seed, and as they mature, children will be able to implement them over time.

This week, in addition to getting you to practise these strategies with your child, I'd like to challenge you with some exercises to reflect on emotional regulation in general.

✓ Can you identify your own emotions at different times? Do you tend to feel one emotion more than another? What is it?

✓ Have you noticed whether these particular emotions affect you? What about your child?

✓ What strategies do you use to regulate your emotions?

✓ Think of three new strategies, after today's session, that you could implement for yourself.

Session | 4

Positive Thinking Module

1. Welcoming participants

The fourth module of this programme explores a core topic – positive thinking. This core skill is introduced slowly to allow the content to be absorbed as required and in a slow-paced manner. Positive thinking is the basis for depression prevention in children and adults alike. Mastering the concept of positive self-talk will ensure children are able to process information in a positive way; however, due to the age of the children, this module may need to be adapted and/or built on over time.

As this is the fourth session, the children should be able to recognise each other and recall their names. The facilitator will ensure that the group continues to be a safe and warm place and will welcome the children back for this session. As the final part of the welcome, the previous session and the skills learnt will be summarised and children will have the opportunity to ask questions or share examples of their 'successes'.

'Hi everyone, welcome back to *Healthy Mindsets for Little Kids*. I'd like to take a minute to go around the circle and ask everyone what they thought of last week's session. What do you remember about what we learnt?'

✓ Housekeeping refresher (toilets, rules and names)

✓ Purpose of session today

✓ Thank participants for feedback about last week.

---

2. Introductory activity

The facilitator will introduce the topic of positive thinking and the notion that 'happy thoughts' have the potential to lead people to feel happier. This occurs by transforming 'dark and gloomy' thoughts into 'bright and bubbly' thoughts. The introductory activity will involve using 'Bear cards' (or any other expression cards). The facilitator will spread them either on the ground or on a table. The children are then asked to choose a card which represents the way

they routinely view things as they occur to them (i.e. angry, scared, unsure, confident, happy etc.). Due to the age of the children, specific examples should be given, for instance, 'How did you feel about attending your first *Healthy Mindsets for Little Kids* session?' or 'How did you feel about your lunch today?', and then comment on how each child and each parent felt different, emphasising we each have our own way of interpreting events.

'Thank you all for this. I look forward to having more fun with you, and to do that today we're going to do an activity. Today's session is on learning to use 'bright and bubbly' thoughts, the thoughts that make us feel nice and fuzzy inside. I'm going to spread some cards on the floor and when I'm done, I'm going to ask all of you to take one card that represents how you felt about attending your first *Healthy Mindsets for Little Kids* session/how you felt about your lunch today?'

> ✓ Thank children for participating
>
> ✓ Reinforce purpose of session today (positive thinking)
>
> ✓ Bear card activity.

3. Why do we feel like that?

The facilitator will introduce the first topic – explaining reasons people may feel sad/angry/negative about things. This should be explained slowly and clearly as those concepts can be difficult to grasp for children. Facilitators are encouraged to use humour in their tone and/or their wording to entertain the children during the conversation. At the end of this session, parents will be asked to volunteer in role playing 'dark and gloomy' vs. 'bright and bubbly', and this should be an opportunity for more fun for the participants in volunteering their own parent. The facilitator will start with quick definitions. To allow children to focus, hand gestures will be used when discussing 'bright and bubbly' thoughts (thumbs up) and 'dark and gloomy' thoughts (thumbs down). Children will be encouraged to use these through the whole programme to really cement the visuals.

Examples of 'dark and gloomy' thoughts include things like:

- Having a 'sad' view of ourselves (I am silly; I am too little etc.)

- Having a 'sad' view of things happening (this is terrible, or the worst thing possible).

Examples of 'bright and bubbly' thoughts include things like:

- Having a 'happy' view of ourselves (I am awesome; I am smart, or kind)

- Having a 'happy' view of things happening (It's not the end of the world; I should be grateful).

'There are a few reasons why some people might feel down about things while other people may not be as sad in the same situation. The first reason may be that they have a sad way of thinking about themselves. Another reason might be that they have a sad way of looking at things. So, what we want to do is practise using 'bright and bubbly' thoughts as much as we can. Now, who would like to see our parents practise this?'

ACTIVITY 1

Select two pairs of parents/carers and allocate them one of these scenarios. Parents should role play a version of this, using dark and gloomy thoughts (ensuring humour and exaggerated actions to get children engaged) and one version using bright and bubbly thoughts (again, using entertaining actions).

- Starting at a new school

- Opening their lunchbox/snack box

- Meeting new friends

- Learning a new instrument

- Trying a new sport

- Not being able to get a new toy/treat

- Not being invited to a party.

DISCUSSION

Which thoughts do you think made our parents feel happier? How do you know? Which thoughts will you try to practise?

✓ Happy thoughts help us feel happy

✓ We all have times where it's hard to think happy thoughts

✓ Children should be reminded of our last session on emotional regulation and invited to utilise some of these strategies.

4. How to create bright and bubbly thoughts

This section should be an expansion of last week's module on feelings and emotional regulation. Children and their parents should be invited to group in pairs and discuss some of things they implemented to feel calm and happy since the last week. The facilitator should go around the room and encourage pairs to recollect moments this week where children and their parents attempted to make themselves feel good or use self-care as per last week's session. The facilitator should praise parents/children for their hard work and show interest in any success stories.

'Now that we've started talking about some of the things we've practised this week to feel positive, I'd like you and your mum/dad to talk to each other about something you did this week that made you feel really good and happy. How did you know it made you feel happy? When we're finished, we might be able to share our cool adventure with the group.'

The facilitator will then assist the group in reforming and invite each child–parent pair to describe a warm and positive activity they attempted and encourage the rest of the group to consider new activities to foster emotional regulation and positive thinking. Parents should be encouraged to commit to new positive strategies with their child.

> 'Bright and bubbly thoughts can help us feel better about things, and today we spoke about ways we could change our dark and gloomy thoughts to happy thoughts. What kind of things will you try this week with Mum or Dad?'

DISCUSSION

What did we practise this week that helped us feel happy? How did you know you felt happy?
Could this also help us create 'bright and bubbly' thoughts?

ACTIVITY 2: CHILD–PARENT DEBRIEFING

> ✓ Come back as a group and share
>
> ✓ Group debriefing on new ideas for emotional regulation and positive thinking ideas to try.

Closing activity: 'Everything is awesome' disco

Participants will be invited to dance to fun and happy songs with their friends and their parents. Songs can be chosen from a wide variety of sources, and should be attractive to children. The facilitator may have blown up balloons for children to tap in the air as they're dancing, as well as using small disco lights if they are available. This activity should only last for a few songs and be a catalyst for parent–child bonding and support in creating bright and bubbly thoughts safely.

The purpose of the activity is to demonstrate an activity that may make the children feel happy, assist parents in facilitating this in their children and providing an age-appropriate activity for participants that illustrates that 'everything can be awesome'.

RESOURCES NEEDED

- Small disco lights (optional)

- Music/songs ('Everything is awesome' works well with the topic)

- Balloons to blow and tap to the music. Ensure there are enough for the whole group.

Closing down the session

The facilitator will summarise the lesson and activity with the participants, building on what they shared and expressed. At the end of this session, children should be aware that 'bright and bubbly' thoughts are great to have, and be reminded of ways to invite them along with the help of their parents/carers.

ZOE THE ZEBRA SOMETIMES HAS OPPOSITE FEELINGS, LIKE HER STRIPES!

SESSION 4: PARENTS' CORNER

'BRIGHT AND BUBBLY THOUGHTS!'

Today we discussed generating 'bright and bubbly' thoughts and avoiding 'dark and gloomy' thoughts. For some parents, depression may be something they have experience of themselves or in their families, therefore it is important to master these early skills. I would invite you to seek support if depression is an issue that affects you as there are lots of positive strategies available.

In the meantime, today, we have encouraged children to recognise positive thoughts and named a few ideas to generate them. To follow on from this session, I would like you to help your child identify bright and bubbly thoughts and praise them when selecting them.

This week, in addition to getting you to discuss your child's positive thoughts and emotional regulation strategies with them, I'd like to challenge you with some exercises to reflect on bright and bubbly attitude in general.

✓ Can you identify your own thinking pattern? How do you feel about it?

✓ Can you think of ways your thinking patterns could influence your child's thinking?

✓ What kind of strategies could you implement as a family to increase the bright and bubbly thoughts?

✓ What kind of support could you facilitate or promote with your child to help them feel positive about themselves and events happening around them?

Session | 5

Communication and Body Language Module

1. Welcoming participants

The fifth module of the programme is on communication, both from a verbal and body language point of view. These core skills are introduced today but will need to be reinforced throughout the rest of the programme as well as at home. Mastering the concept of communication is important (for children as well as teenagers and adults) to process and transmit information in a constructive way; however, due to the age of the participants, this module may need to be adapted and/or built on over time.

As per every session, the facilitator will ensure that the group continues to be a safe and warm place and will welcome the children back for this session. Finally, the previous session and the skills learnt will be summarised and children will have the opportunity to ask questions or share examples of their 'successes'.

> 'Hi everyone, welcome back to *Healthy Mindsets for Little Kids*. I'd like to take a minute to go around the circle and ask everyone what they thought of last week's session. What do you remember about what we learnt?'

✓ Housekeeping refresher (toilets, rules and names)

✓ Purpose of session today

✓ Thank participants for feedback about last week.

---

2. Introductory activity

The facilitator will introduce the topic of 'manners'. Though the topic is on communication, some younger children may not be able to understand its concept and therefore other terms may be used to represent this (manners, happy/angry faces/words etc.) and the notion that 'good manners/communication' have the potential to let people communicate better and more positively. This occurs by transforming abrupt words, and/or 'angry/sad' body language, into polite and friendly ones. The introductory activity will involve using 'Bear cards' (or any other expression cards). The facilitator will spread them either on the ground or on a table. The children are then asked to choose a card, which represents different body language as called out by the facilitator (i.e. angry, sad, happy, quiet, excited etc.). The purpose is to introduce the topic and assist children in identifying various body language and their associated meanings.

> 'Today's session is on learning to use "manners" and positive communication. Both in the way we speak, and in the way our bodies speak. For our first activity, I'm going to spread some cards on the floor and when I'm done, let's pick cards that represent someone [insert emotion].'

- ✓ Thank children for participating
- ✓ Reinforce purpose of session today (positive thinking)
- ✓ Bear card activity.

3. My good manners

The facilitator will introduce the first topic, which explains what manners are. The facilitator will go around the group and ask each child and parent to name something that shows good manners. Examples include:

- Please
- Thank you
- May/could/shall/can I?
- Waiting turns
- Listening to someone when they're speaking
- Smiling
- Soft gestures
- Carrying someone's bag
- Offering to help
- Holding someone's hand while they're crossing the road
- Helping Mum or Dad do the dishes/fold clothes/empty the bin etc.

'Both our bodies and words can show others good communication and good manners. How do you think you could show Mum or Dad, or your friends and teachers, your lovely manners? Do you see how being able to use manners and communicate well may help with making new friends?'

ACTIVITY 1

Child–parent teams should be formed. Depending on the ages of the children, it may be possible to form child–child and parent–parent teams instead. Each team will attempt to mime a series of actions/situations and the rest of the group will need to guess what these are. The purpose of this activity is to demonstrate how our bodies can communicate information and assist children in reading other people's body language. Some examples of simple mimes might include:

- A car
- An elephant
- A teacher
- Mum/Dad
- A baby
- A kitten/puppy
- A hairdresser
- A soccer player
- A dancer.

Children should be encouraged to pay attention to their body language, their aggressive/passive/assertive presence (within developmental age-appropriate parameters), the actions/movements they're using etc. If child or the group is struggling with guessing the mime, the facilitator may allow the participants to use words. If this is the case, children should be encouraged to pay attention to these and how they may influence others.

DISCUSSION

What did you think of the game? Did any of the actions or words make your character seem friendlier than others?

How do you think these may work in real life?

✓ Manners help us communicate nicely

✓ Body language is another form of talking, and we can make it friendly or angry

✓ Mimes guessing game

ACTIVITY 2

This section should be an expansion of the previous activity. The facilitator should ensure that children are clear about what was taught, including the use of body language and manners. In this activity, children will practise using manners in specific contexts via simple role plays. Pairs will be formed based on the children's ages, needs and personality. For many, parent–child pairs will be the easiest format, however this can be decided at the time.

'Now that we've had lots of fun practising our mimes, let's try to practise our wonderful words. For this next game, we're going to play a guessing game. I'll call out sentences, and you have to guess what words might be polite or good manners to add to these sentences. How does that sound? I'll give you an example right now. If I said, "Give me some milk!" what words would you add or change?' (In this example, the answer could be 'please', 'could you', 'may I have' etc.)

The facilitator will assist the group in coming up with alternatives for each sentence spoken. The idea is to generate good and positive alternatives and to ensure children see the rationale and benefit for these additional words and manners. Sentences can be generated on the spot, and should be developmentally age-appropriate for the participants. For ease, a few examples are listed below:

- I want to go to the zoo
- Be quiet
- Clean up your room
- I received your present
- Don't fight with your brother or sister.

DISCUSSION
How do you think these extra words change the sentences?
Could this work in real life too?

✓ Come back as a group and share
✓ Group debriefing on new ideas for positive communication.

Closing activity: 'Manners' bingo

Participants will be invited to play a manners bingo game. The game has been simplified to take into account the developmental ages of the participants. The rules are simple. Each parent and child will form a team (as some of the children will not be of reading age). The facilitator will call out words as they appear on the reading card (e.g. thank you, please, may I etc.). The parent–child pairs will then need to cross out that word from their card. Options for the game include finishing one (or two) vertical lines, horizontal lines, a diagonal line or the full card. When a pair has finished, they need to call out 'bingo' to win. Small treats or stickers may be used as prizes if chosen. This can be adapted as appropriate with each cohort of participants.

The purpose of the activity is to expose children to words and general good communications skills through this easy and fun game. Parents and children will also bond and work as a team to call out bingo on time. The facilitator will continue to encourage all participants in using their manners through the whole module.

RESOURCES NEEDED

- Bingo caller's card (Appendix 1)
- Bingo cards × 10 (Appendix 2).

Closing down the session

The facilitator will summarise the session and activity with the participants, building on what they shared and expressed. At the end of this session, children should be aware that 'manners' assist with good communication and that both body language and verbal skills are important. The facilitator will invite participants to practise with the help of their parents/carers.

> 'Good manners and friendly body language are awesome at making us and other people feel really positive and send clear messages. What kind of things will you try this week with Mum or Dad, and/or with your friends and teachers?'

CARLISLE THE CROCODILE HAS LEARNT MANNERS AND HOW TO PLAY NICELY TODAY. WHAT ABOUT YOU?

SESSION 5: PARENTS' CORNER

'WATCHING MY MANNERS!'

In some families, manners and good communication are clear and well-articulated. In others, it is harder and a little more inconsistent. Teaching young children good communication skills from an early age is vital and can lead to better social skills and good mental health.

I'd like you to be aware and mindful of your own communication skills this week. Challenge your partner, relatives or friends to communicate positively when they speak in front of your child and make an effort yourself. Encourage your child to practise their manners, and make the whole process fun!

To do this, let me challenge you with the following:

✓ With your child, stand in front of a mirror and practise passive, assertive and aggressive body language. Discuss.

✓ In the car, or while doing mundane activities, sing or list manners until someone runs out of ideas. The last person is the winner.

✓ Record yourself talking to your partner, friend or relative (with their permission) for a set amount of time. Then listen and observe your own communication skills.

✓ Do the same while talking to your child. How do you feel about your communication skills while talking to your child? Surprised? Happy? Unhappy?

✓ Praise them for using good verbal and body language skills.

✓ Lead by example!

BINGO CALLER'S CARD

Thank you	May I	Thanks
Could I	Can I	Lovely
Manners	Smiles	Thumbs up!

APPENDIX 2: Bingo Cards

BINGO CARD

Lovely	Manners	Smiles
Thank you	Can I	Thumbs up!
May I	Could I	Thanks

✓

BINGO CARD

Manners	Thanks	Smiles
Could I	Thank you	Can I
Lovely	May I	Thumbs up!

BINGO CARD

Thank you	Manners	Thumbs up!
May I	Could I	Smiles
Thanks	Can I	Lovely

✓

BINGO CARD

May I	Manners	Thumbs up!
Can I	Lovely	Smiles
Thanks	Could I	Thank you

BINGO CARD

Thank you	Can I	Manners
Lovely	May I	Thumbs up!
Smiles	Thanks	Could I

✓

BINGO CARD

Lovely	Can I	May I
Thanks	Could I	Manners
Thumbs up!	Thank you	Smiles

BINGO CARD

Smiles	Thank you	Could I
May I	Thanks	Manners
Thumbs up!	Can I	Lovely

✓

BINGO CARD

Thumbs up!	Thank you	Smiles
Manners	Could I	Lovely
May I	Can I	Thanks

BINGO CARD

Smiles	Lovely	Thank you
Could I	Thanks	Can I
Thumbs up!	Manners	May I

✓

BINGO CARD

May I	Could I	Thank you
Manners	Smiles	Thumbs up!
Lovely	Can I	Thanks

Session | 6

Social Skills Module

1. Welcoming participants

The sixth module of the programme looks at social skills: more specifically empathy and managing conflict. Empathy is an important skill that allows children and adults alike to develop the ability to put themselves in someone else's shoes, to imagine another person's perspective and to open their minds to the idea that others may have different opinions, thoughts, values or ideas. Whilst young children may struggle at truly showing empathy and understanding the position of a third party due to their developmental needs, teaching them empathy and conflict resolution as they grow up is an important part of healthy social skills and a good start to future learning.

'I hope that everyone has a great week! I'd like to hear how your week went. (*The facilitator will go around the group and ask each child about the last few days. Then, he or she will reflect on the disclosure to introduce the notion of empathy and role model feedback skills.*) We've heard lots of different things which happened to us and to our friends today. How do you think you'd feel if these things had happened to you? (*Once the children have expressed their thoughts, the facilitator will introduce this week's topic.*) Being able to understand how our friends might feel is really helpful in being a good friend. Today's lesson is on understanding other people's points of views, and on managing the times where we might disagree.'

✓ Purpose of session today

✓ Thank children for their attendance.

ACTIVITY 1

The facilitator will further introduce the topic of empathy, though the language may need to be adapted to suit the participants' developmental levels. For this activity, the facilitator will read a story to the participants. The story will be in two parts. The first section will portray a character undergoing difficulty and the children will be tasked to imagine what that would feel like, and some of the things that might be helpful to that character. The second part will be designed to finish the scenario on a positive note, and for children to process and discuss their thoughts and feelings about the new story development. At the end of the story, parent–child pairs will split from the group and spend some time in discussing the story, and answering questions from the worksheet at the end of this module. Due to the age of the children, in most cases, the parents will write. Parents and facilitators will encourage the participants through this activity.

'Today's session is on imagining what people might feel when things happen to them. Most times, when we're able to understand what our friends or family feels, we might be able to help or show something we call "empathy". Like I explained earlier, that means our ability to imagine what other people might be going through. What about I read you a story, and in a minute, your mum/dad and you will talk about the story and try to answer questions about it. Would that be okay?'

✓ Thank children and parents for participating

✓ Reinforce purpose of section (empathy)

✓ Story telling activity (story and questions can be found at the end of the module).

---

2. Getting along!

The facilitator will introduce the second topic today, which is conflict management. This module will discuss ways to manage conflicts and emotions during times of conflict in children in a way that fits their developmental age and situation. Strategies will be brainstormed and practised in this section, and parents will be invited to contribute and guide the conversation with personalised examples about their children if suitable and appropriate.

'Today we learnt that when we try to imagine what others feel, we can help them better and become a better friend. But sometimes, friends or family members might still argue or disagree. That's normal and that's okay. It would be good to learn ways to get along with others. Who can tell me things they've done to get along with others?'

The facilitator, with the help of parents, will assist participants in brainstorming actions and ideas. Some examples may include:

- Taking our turn
- Using manners
- Listening to our friends
- Using words to express how we feel
- Showing respect
- Imagining how other people might feel
- Helping find solutions
- Listening without interrupting
- Saying sorry if you did something to someone else by accident
- Following the rules.

The facilitator should praise the children for coming up with these ideas. He or she may give them suggestions if they struggle coming up with their own. Parents should assist children in recalling events where these strategies were used in their family and a discussion about the benefit of these should occur now.

DISCUSSION

Tell us about a time where you used some of these strategies? Did it help you and/or your friend?

Why do you think it is important to resolve conflict when we can?

3. ABCD of conflict resolution in children

The facilitator will introduce the ABCD of conflict management for young children. This should be simplified and explained in a way that makes sense and can be utilised in practice by the participants. This is a four-step process that children can use with support from an adult to resolve conflict as it arises. This should be used in conjunction with the other strategies learnt in this book over the last 5 weeks.

ABCD MODEL

A	Ask what the problem is
B	Brainstorm solutions
C	Choose a solution to try
D	Do it! And with a smile!

ACTIVITY 2

The facilitator will introduce the ABCD concept and give examples as he or she explains each step, in a way that makes sense to the children. Through these examples, scenarios will be presented to each child–parent pair for role playing. This should be done in a play-like manner and children should not be forced to role play. Instead, it should be offered like a game and praise, clapping and encouragements should be high. In the event of children feeling a little shy or unwilling to participate, parents could team up and role play the scenarios, with the children having a minimal role. Each step (A, B, C and D) should be role modelled until the children understand these and are able to retain them.

Examples of scenarios include:

- Your friend is using a toy you would like

- Your friend grabbed your pencils without asking

- Your brother/sister won't let you change the TV channel

- Your mum/dad asked you to eat your dinner and you don't like it

- You went to wear your favourite shirt, but it's in the wash

- You would like to join a group of friends to play at school, but you're afraid to ask

- You would like to play Monopoly but your cousin wants to play Jenga.

DISCUSSION

Who can tell me what ABC and D stand for?
Did we practise these well in our role plays today?
How could we practise them in real life?

✓ ABCDs can help us resolve arguments with our friends and our family

✓ There are lots of ways we can learn to get along with others

✓ Role playing activity.

Closing activity: 'Jenga' or similar simple group game

The facilitator will invite the children to play a simple game of Jenga or similar. The game should have simple rules, not require resources and be time efficient. The purpose of the activity is to expose children to social skills such as taking turns, using manners, considering their peers and their peers' needs. The facilitator will praise the children through the game and role model conflict resolution skills (ABCD) through the activity.

RESOURCES NEEDED

- Game (Jenga, dominoes, chain the monkey or similar simple game).

Closing down the session

The facilitator will summarise the lesson and activity with the participants, building on what they shared and expressed as per the previous modules. By now, the lessons should be starting to complement each other and the learning should add on to the learning from previous sessions. At the end of this module, children should understand the concept of empathy, to some extent, depending on their developmental age ('What would I be feeling if I were in my friend's situation?'). The story and the practice of the ABCDs will assist children in developing empathy and conflict management skills. These will need to be practised as children mature and/or they 'forget' these exercises without the reminders.

'Today we learnt about Elijah and Samantha's story and how Samantha was able to imagine what Elijah might be feeling. Thinking about what others could be feeling will help us be good friends. Today, we also learnt about the ABCD to resolve little fights we might be having. This is a cool way to be a good friend too. I'm going to practise being a good friend this week. What about you?'

DANIEL THE DOG KNOWS HOW TO HELP HIS FRIENDS. I KNOW YOU DO, TOO.

SESSION 6: PARENTS' CORNER

'BEING A GOOD FRIEND!'

This session introduced some very important topics, including empathy and conflict resolution. Young children can struggle with these, particularly the first time these concepts are applied in practice due to their developmental needs. This is why it is paramount to practise and reinforce these. I'd like to invite you to role model these skills in your daily life, with your child, other children, other parents etc. Make it routine to role model empathy and conflict resolution in your household!

Further to this, let me challenge you with the following:

✓ Consider your own empathy levels when hearing stories from friends and relatives. Does this come easily? Is this difficult?

✓ How have you shown sympathy and support to others in the past?

✓ How do you resolve conflict with your peers? Spouse? Friends? Children?

✓ Role model today's session with story books and/or stories your children might share after school. Help them problem solve and consider others' perspectives.

STORY TELLING: THE BIRTHDAY PARTY

PART ONE

Once upon a time, there was a little boy. His name was Elijah. When he turned 6, his mummy told him he couldn't have a birthday party this year because his baby brother, Jett, was only a newborn and needed lots of attention.

Elijah was very sad. He really wanted a birthday party to invite all his best friends and eat some yummy chocolate cake.

That morning, Elijah went to school sad. His shoulders were droopy. His smile was upside down. He dragged his feet all the way to his class, crossing the school without saying hello to his teacher, Miss Naude, or his best friend, Samantha.

Samantha trotted after him. 'Elijah! Elijah! Why are you sad?'

Elijah shrugged. 'Because of my silly baby brother, I can't have a birthday party.'

A tear slid down Elijah's cheek.

PART TWO

'Awww, don't cry, Elijah. I think I have an idea!' Samantha said, before she ran off to their classroom.

Elijah frowned. What could Samantha be thinking? Could she have thought of a good idea? He wondered what it could be!

Five minutes later, Samantha and their teacher Miss Naude approached Elijah. Miss Naude and Samantha had big, bright smiles on their faces.

Miss Naude knelt in front of Elijah. 'Elijah, how would you like to have a class birthday party?'

Elijah looked up, his eyes twinkling. 'Really? I could have a class party? With chocolate cake?'

Samantha clapped her hand and laughed. 'Yes, Elijah. Miss Naude said we could have chocolate cake!'

STORY TELLING WORKSHEET: The Birthday Party

PART ONE

What was the name of the little boy? _____

How old was he? _____

Why couldn't he have a birthday party? _____

_____

How did the little boy feel in the first part of the story? _____

_____

_____

_____

How do you know? What made you think he felt this way? _____

_____

_____

_____

How do you think you would have felt if you were the little boy? _____

_____

_____

_____

PART TWO

What was the name of the little girl? _____

Was the little girl a good friend? _____

How do you know? What made you say that? _____

_____

_____

_____

Why do you think she wanted to be a good friend to Elijah? _____

_____

_____

_____

How could you be a good friend too? _____

_____

_____

_____

Session | 7

Learning about Discipline Module

1. Welcoming participants

The seventh module of the programme is on discipline and on 'green' and 'red' behaviours. It is aimed at both parents and children; the emphasis is on working out healthy boundaries, behaviours and consequences.

In this session, the facilitator's role modelling is vital. Some carers may have had poor examples themselves and/or not know how to manage some aspect of parenting and/or discipline with their children. The opportunity to discuss positive strategies and to foster a safe environment for the group to discuss these challenges is paramount.

'Hi everyone, I hope you all had a wonderful week and that you're ready for this week's module! Today we're going to talk about our "green" behaviours, our "orange" and our "red" behaviours. Your teacher may have talked about these behaviours at kindy or preschool. Who can tell me what they think "green", "orange" and "red" behaviours are?'

Once the facilitator has allowed the group to guess what these behaviours are, he or she may move on to explain why they are important to recognise and the purpose of the lesson: to increase our green behaviours, manage our orange behaviours and address children's red behaviour in a way that is consistent, fair and efficient.

✓ Purpose of session today

✓ Thank participants for their attendance.

ACTIVITY 1

The facilitator will further present the topic of behaviours and introduce an activity to get the children and their carers/parents to come up with examples of each type of behaviour to solidify the group's understanding of these. Due to the age of the children, positive behaviours will be labelled 'green' while negative behaviours will be labelled 'red'.

For the purpose of this exercise, the facilitator will prepare two large posters. A green one titled 'Green choices' and a red one titled 'Red choices'. The facilitator will have prepared the behaviour cards (Appendices 1 and 2 at the end of this module). It may help to add Velcro dots on the posters, or blue tack for the cards to stick to them: facilitators may be creative and utilise these as they are practical in their groups. Children will then be invited to take turns at picking a card from a bag/hat and to place the card on the right poster (Green/Red). Each child will be praised for their turn. In cases where a child may be unsure, their carer and/or facilitator may assist.

'How about we play a game about green and red behaviours? Each of you will take turns at picking a card, and then you'll get to place it on the "green choice" or "red choice" poster. If you'd like, you could even give us an example of a time where you used these green behaviours at home or at school. If you pick a "red" choice, you could tell us why you think it's one that we should try to avoid. Don't worry. If you have any trouble, we're all here to help. Who would like to start?'

✓ Thank children and parents for participating

✓ Reinforce purpose of section (green and red behaviours)

✓ Green and red card behaviours (Appendices 1 and 2).

---

2. High Five!

The facilitator will introduce the concept of 'High Five' behaviour management strategy. A majority of children may be using these at kindy or at school, however some may not. Some of the parents and/or carers may not be familiar with them at all and therefore the reminder will be useful to everyone in the group. While explaining the steps as per the instructions below, the facilitator should ensure that he or she presents these steps in an interactive way, allowing the children to guess them and making it a fun and non-threatening activity.

'Who at their school has used "High Five"? *(The facilitator will allow children to speak about their current knowledge of the High Five model before continuing.)* High Five shows us what to do when our friends or other people are using red behaviours around us. *(The facilitator will hold their hand up and use their fingers to illustrate all the five points. He or she will invite all participants to do the same.)* The first thing we should do if someone is doing something we don't like, is to use our words and let them know. Do you remember the modules from Carlisle the Crocodile and Daniel the Dog? We learnt how to use manners and ways to talk friendly. So, the first step of high five is "talk friendly". The second is "talk firmly", the third is to ignore the red behaviour from our friend and the fourth is to walk away if ignoring is not working. And finally, one more step. Who can tell me what the last step might be?'

The facilitator will then hand the worksheet featuring the High Five hand to the participants and allow the children to colour it in while the group continues to discuss the five steps and how to put then in action.

DISCUSSION

Who has ever tried to ignore a red behaviour? What happened? Was it easy?

Who has any idea of what talking friendly to someone might sound like? What about talking firmly? Who would like to show us an example?

Who would you tell if your friend's red behaviour continued?

✓ Thank children and parents for participating

✓ High Five model discussion

✓ Worksheet 1.

---

3. My house rules

This section is about parents as much as it is about the children. It is extremely important that the facilitator manages any tension and insecurities in the room that may result in poor emotional regulation after the group. This section should be about understanding the importance of fair consequences as a result of green and red behaviours. To ensure the children do not feel intimidated or 'in trouble', positive reinforcement should be discussed as much as consequences for negative behaviours.

'I'm sure you've noticed in your class at school that when people use red behaviours too often, they may get a warning. Sometimes the warning leads to time out, or a special quiet task. When children use green behaviours, they might get a sticker, a special reward or an award. These are called consequences. And even adults have them. For example, if your mum or dad arrive at work late every morning, they may have to stay back late at night to make up the time, or if they don't follow the road rules in their car, they may get a fine. Consequences are normal and apply to everyone.

Today, I'd like to talk about a chart that you and your family could maybe use at home to help with having less red behaviours and more green behaviours. It wouldn't have to be just for the children. It could be for your brothers or sisters, and even mum or dad!

Working with your mum or dad and using the worksheet I'm about to give you (Worksheet 2), I'd like you to think of three or four rules for your family and what rewards might work, or what consequences might be fair.'

If parent–child pairs need assistance, the following examples may be given:

- Setting the table

- Making your bed/cleaning your room

- Doing work/homework

- Eating dinner

- Helping with dishes

- Brushing your teeth right away

- Being kind/being helpful.

Consequences should be age-appropriate, fair and consistent. It is the role of the facilitator during this session to assist parents with establishing positive natural and logical consequences which are anger-free, reasonable, and sensible and also include positive reinforcements to balance things out.

DISCUSSION

Do you think consequences are fair? What about rewards?

Why can't we allow everyone to show red behaviours when they feel like it? What would happen if we did?

How do you think your house rules might help the whole family?

✓ Thank children and parents for participating

✓ My house rules and consequences discussion

✓ Worksheet 2: My house rules.

4. Helping me stay away from red behaviours

The facilitator will introduce brief strategies that may assist children in regulating when engaging in red behaviours. However, these will be discussed in more depth in the next chapter on anger management, and this section should only be an introduction to these due to time constraints and the attention span/needs of the young participants.

DISCUSSION

What kind of things would help you remember not to use red behaviours?
What would help you in feeling good and using more green behaviours?

'Some kids find it helpful to take a time out when they're feeling annoyed or angry. Things like taking deep breaths or going for a walk might work. Lots of children find that getting hugs or playing a nice calm game might help them focus on green behaviours again. What works for you?'

The facilitator will allow parents and children to take turns at naming one or two things that would help them focus on green behaviours and let them know that they will be learning about these next week.

'We also learnt about the High Five model – who can remind me what these five steps are? We also discussed house rules, consequences and rewards that might be fair for your family. So for our last activity of the day, what about we make up a consequence ladder that will show us all the steps from a warning to a reward and help us keep on track?'

Closing activity: Consequence ladder chart poster

The facilitator will invite the participants to create personalised charts about behaviours in general. Some pairs may choose to target a chore or a behaviour (manners, sharing, cleaning room, eating breakfast etc.), while other may choose to keep the poster more general (red, orange, green) and have the consequences progress to rewards through the height of the chart (e.g. warning, time out, polite request for extra time on the iPad or other type of reward).

RESOURCES NEEDED

- Large cardboard sheet/posters – one per parent–child pair (red section, orange section and green sections should appear evenly on the side of the poster to allow parent–child pairs to decide and illustrate natural and fair consequences of behaviours as they progress from red, to orange and green.)

- Felt pens/crayons etc.

- Glitter pens, stickers etc.

Closing down the session

The facilitator will summarise the lesson and activity with the participants, building on what they shared and expressed as per the previous modules. As advised in the previous modules, it would be expected that the lessons should have started to complement each other, and the learning should add on to the previous learning. It is important for the facilitator to remind participants of how all the skills taught in this programme need to be practised and used together to improve the new teachings.

At the end of this module, children should understand the concept of red and green behaviours as well as the notion of consequences and rewards. Though parents and children would have discussed natural consequences, for the last exercise of this module, we'll focus on a consequence ladder that includes a wide range of reinforcements from warning to rewards, with a focus on positive behaviours.

'Today we learnt about red and green behaviours. We discussed that when we behave a particular way, we may receive a warning or a consequence, or a reward. This is pretty clever, and I'm definitely going to work hard at getting my green behaviours shining. What about you?'

MATTY THE MONKEY CAN BE CHEEKY. WILL YOU TEACH HIM GREEN BEHAVIOURS?

SESSION 7: PARENTS' CORNER

'RIGHT AND WRONG BEHAVIOURS!'

Discipline and parenting is hard work! There are a few things you can work on, on a personal level and as a family, to ensure children are guided into 'green' behaviours.

Let me invite you to consider the following:

> ✓ What kind of routines do you have available for your child? Are they structured or more ad-hoc? How could you change it to ensure their routines for homework, sports, bedtime etc. are consistent and stress-free?
>
> ✓ Talk it out! Do you explain your reasons to your child? Children are very smart! They are more likely to listen to instructions when they understand the reasoning behind them.
>
> ✓ Pick natural consequences when you can and avoid extreme knee-jerk reactions that are impossible to implement or not in proportion with the behaviour. For example, if your child keeps losing their hat at school, a natural consequence might be that they're required to play in the undercover area for a while.
>
> ✓ Praise good behaviours when you catch them. Nothing beats positive reinforcements.
>
> ✓ Teach your child problem-solving! There's often a simple solution to their issues. Helping them work this out will lead to more green behaviours.
>
> ✓ Be a role model. Children learn by watching the adults around them. If they see you behave in a negative way, they're likely to model that. If they see you behave in a positive and constructive way, they're more likely to aim for it.

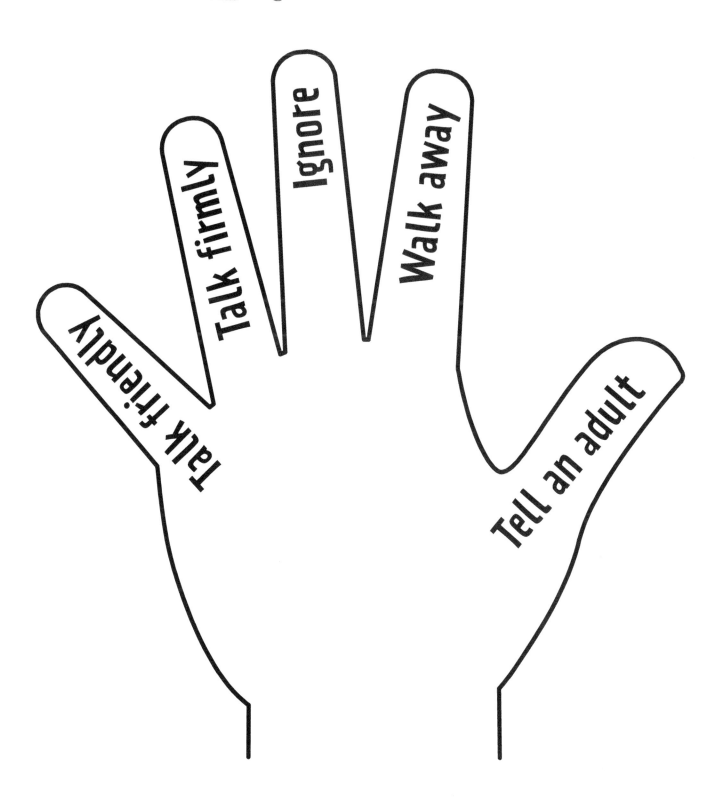

APPENDIX 1: Green behaviour cards

Be kind

Work as a team

Use my words

Take turns

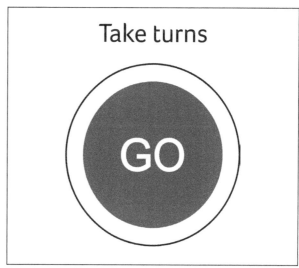

Do my best

Follow directions

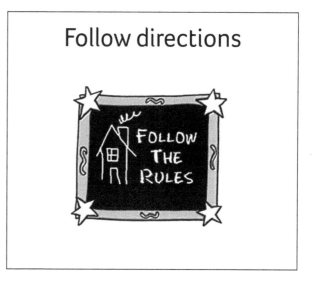

Clean up my room

Listen

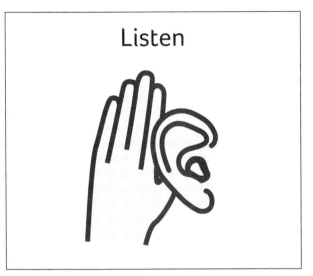

Sit properly

Throw away rubbish

Share

Use manners

APPENDIX 2: Red behaviour cards

Angry bodies

Hit others

Mean words

Throw things on the floor

Yell

Break things

Annoy others 	**Run inside** 
Tell a lie 	**Not following directions** 
Being selfish 	**Talk over others** 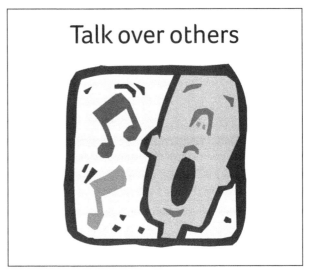

Session | 8

Anger Management Module

1. Welcoming participants

The eighth module of *Healthy Mindsets for Little Kids* is on regulating emotions, and in particular anger management. In this session, the facilitator will assist children in understanding that feeling angry is okay, as long as they do not use 'red' behaviours (as discussed in the last module). As per all modules, role modelling from the facilitator and the carers is vital. Things like quiet and calm voices, warm body language and respectful participation will need to be agreed upon at the beginning of this programme.

Some families may be involved with individuals who may display anger management issues and, therefore, it is important for the group to feel safe and able to discuss the content of this module without feeling on 'show' or 'judged' as they attempt these new skills.

'Hi everyone, I hope you had another great week, and that you're ready to have fun today! Today we're going to talk about our angry feelings and what happens when we feel them. We'll learn about things we could do to feel calm and learn to use "green" behaviours even when we feel angry inside our bellies.'

Once the facilitator has introduced the topic of anger management, he or she will make the participants feel comfortable and begin the session.

✓ Purpose of session today

✓ Thank participants for their attendance.

ACTIVITY 1

The facilitator will spread Bear cards on the ground (any types of emotion cards are suitable). The cards should highlight a wide range of facial expressions and body language. He or she will then ask participants to pick one they believe highlights a character who is feeling angry and ask each person to explain why they chose that particular card. Then each participant will be invited to provide an example to the group of one time they felt angry and what occurred.

'Let's start this session by playing a game. I'm going to spread some cards on the floor, and I'm going to ask you to choose one that shows an angry bear [or whatever other character is showcased]. If that's okay with you, tell us why you think this might be the case? And when you're done, we'd love to hear about a time where you felt angry and what happened then.'

Parents or carers will be invited to take turns before their children in view of role modelling the activity. The facilitator will ensure that children are assisted in keeping their examples reasonably short and light.

> ✓ Thank children and parents for participating
>
> ✓ Reinforce purpose of section (anger management)
>
> ✓ Bear card activities.

2. Annabella's mad day

The facilitator will introduce the story of Annabella (Worksheet 1) to open up a discussion on anger and appropriate ways to manage angry feelings. There are two parts to this story. Part 1 highlights Annabella's red behaviour as a result of feeling angry, while Part 2 highlights the green behaviours Annabella chose. The purpose of this activity is to facilitate the children's realisation and acknowledgement that there are better ways to manage their anger.

The facilitator will ensure all children feel included and none of the children feel targeted. This story, like Elijah's story in module 6, should be interactive, fun and inviting to the children. Participants should be able to guess some of the answers as the facilitator tells the story. Parents and carers should be encouraged to balance the children's enthusiasm so that they're participating while still turning turns and listening adequately.

> 'How would you feel if I read you an awesome story today? It's the story of Annabella and how she had to learn about her feelings. There are two parts to this story and you'll have to guess what behaviours she used, and tell us which ones worked best. I'd love you to help me during the story by guessing some of the missing words and/or what you think might be happening. Yeah?'

Once the facilitator has finished reading the story (Worksheet 1) and the children and their carers are well involved in the process, a discussion on anger and anger strategies will occur as a group. The 'Harry the Hedgehog' colouring sheet may be handed to each participant to assist with managing the attention span of the young children. An emphasis on the fact that anger is not a negative emotion should follow. The distinction between the normal emotion (anger) and someone's choice of behaviour (green vs. red) will be paramount.

DISCUSSION

How can you tell that Annabella was angry? What about you? How do *you* know when you're angry?

Is it okay to be angry?

Was it easy to guess which behaviours were red, and which ones were green?

What kind of green behaviours do you think you could use when feeling angry?

✓ Thank children and parents for participating

✓ Worksheet 1 'Annabella's mad day'.

3. What about when I get angry?

In this section, the facilitator will personalise anger management to children. The facilitator will encourage parents to get involved and role model their own anger management strategies. Again, this section is important and the value of positive role modelling is vital.

The facilitator will invite the children to reflect on their own bodies as they feel anger. Using Worksheet 2 (Angry feelings in my body), children and their parents will split into pairs and focus on each child's description of angry feelings, where they are located in their body and what they may feel like (belly ache, headache, sweating, sore voice etc.). It is important to take this opportunity to continue to acknowledge anger as a normal and healthy emotion.

Once each parent–child pair has finished, the facilitator will invite them to discuss green behaviours together as discussed over the last few weeks, and name which ones might be suitable for each family/child. Then, they will write three green behaviours on the worksheet and agree to try.

Some examples may include:

- Reading a book

- Playing Lego

- Playing with electronics

- Having a bath or a shower

- Walking the dog

- Getting a hug from Mum or Dad

- Drinking a hot chocolate

- Using our words to express our feelings

- Watching TV

- Playing with friends or neighbours

- Listening to music.

Once this activity has been completed, the group will form and each pair will be invited to share their worksheet if they so choose.

DISCUSSION

Where do anger feelings travel in your body? What do these feel like?
What green behaviour did you and Mum/Dad choose to try?

✓ Thank children and parents for participating

✓ Worksheet 2: 'Angry feelings in my body'.

Closing activity: 'Calming down box'

The facilitator will invite the participants to create personalised boxes filled with safe sensory materials. While this activity is done, informal praise and discussion on the children's green behaviours will occur and an ongoing commitment to work on positive anger management strategies from children and their parents should be encouraged. Lots of planning and resources will be required for this activity to be successful.

RESOURCES NEEDED

- A small decorative box per child. It is not recommended to use thin boxes (e.g. cereal packets) but rather gift-type boxes from a discount store to avoid early breakage

- Soft, prickly or different types of materials (donations from a craft store are good ideas)

- A small music toy

- A strong-smelling cloth (a couple of drops of mint or lemon oil works well)

- A small notepad with stickers and/or crayons

- A small balloon filled with rice

- A squeeze toy (ensure safety and that it won't burst)

- Family photos

- Letters from friends or family

- Shells, leaves or other memorabilia from positive memories

- School awards etc.

- Any other personalised items that might help children regulate.

Closing down the session

The facilitator will summarise the lesson and activity with the participants. Each child should understand that anger is a normal emotion and have started to consider some green behaviours they could engage in. Some examples should have been discussed and parents should have made notes of how they could support their children in attempting these. It is important that these sessions do not have a punitive vibe but a positive one.

'Today we talked about feeling angry and how it is normal. Everybody feels angry at times! It's what we do when we feel angry that matters, and so I'm hoping that with your mum or dad, you'll be able to try lots of green behaviours for when you feel angry. Now, to end today's session, we're going to make a calming down box. We will fill it with lots of safe and nice things that you'll be able to use when you need to calm down.'

HARRY THE HEDGEHOG IS NO LONGER PRICKLY WHEN ANGRY. GOOD JOB HARRY!

SESSION 8: PARENTS' CORNER

'I CAN CALM MYSELF DOWN!'

Anger management is a tricky topic due to the negative connotation it has for people. If we can understand that feeling angry is a normal emotion, then it makes sense that rather than being upset with your child when he or she expresses anger, we might be more inclined to help them choose green behaviours to express their emotions.

However, children learn by watching the adults around them and without positive role modelling, they are bound to use red behaviours or behaviours that cause them problems down the line. Therefore, I would like to encourage you to consider your own anger issues if you have any as well as family strategies to communicate.

Here are some tips to get you started:

✓ Get the whole family on board. Green behaviours are not a 'child' commitment but a whole family commitment.

✓ Grow aware of your own behaviours. Could these be improved? What about the behaviours of your partner, siblings, friends and relatives?

✓ Find green and relaxing activities as a family or on a date with your child. Make it a pleasant moment.

✓ Add to the calming box as you go and encourage your child to use their chosen strategies as needed.

✓

PART ONE

Annabella **ran** through the kitchen and **pushed** her brother, Billy, out of the way as he was standing in front of the cupboard.

'Hey!' he cried, 'it's my bowl!'

Annabella **slammed** the cupboard door hard. She settled at the kitchen bench and poured cereal into the purple bowl. '**Nah. It's mine**.'

Mum rushed in and saw Billy crying. 'What is going on?' she asked.

'Nothing. **He's being a cry baby**,' Annabella answered as she **smirked**.

'Annabella, you know the bowl is mine and I said you could both use it.'

Annabella **threw** her spoon on the floor. '**But I don't like sharing**!'

PART TWO

Annabella **walked quietly** through the kitchen and **smiled** at her brother. 'Good morning, Billy.'

'Hi,' he said, 'I'm having cereals today.'

'Yum. Me too!' Annabella said as she **carefully reached** for the purple bowl.

'Hey! I was going to use this!' Billy cried.

Annabella **stopped** and put the bowl on the bench. 'It was your turn yesterday. Today is my turn, and if you don't share, we **need to ask Mum** to help us sort it out.'

Mum came in and asked, 'What's going on?'

'It's my turn to use your bowl. **Can you help us sort it out**?'

'Thank you, Annabella, for asking for help. Now let's see what we can do here…'

WORKSHEET 2: Angry feelings in my body

Where do you feel your angry feelings?

Session | 9

Anxiety Management Module

1. Welcoming participants

The facilitator will welcome the participants to their ninth session. This module is on anxiety management and strategies for regulating stress in typical childhood situations. Clearly, this module does not cover clinical anxiety in highly acute situations or situations that are beyond 'normal' stressors in children that age; however, these foundation skills are a good start to teach young ones about resilience and strategies they can practise as stressors emerge.

As per some of the other modules, some families may be surrounded by bigger stressors than others (family dynamics, financial stressors, social issues, amongst other things) and the facilitator should be mindful of these and/or triggers that may arise as a result of this session. Further, as per the rest of this book, and due to the age of the children, this module should remain non-threatening, fun and play-based.

'Hi everyone, how are we today? Today, we're going to learn about the butterflies in our bellies when we feel a little stressed or anxious and how we can make them go away. How does that sound?'

Once the facilitator has introduced the topic of anxiety management, he or she will make the participants feel comfortable and begin the session by asking participants about their experience. Props such as butterfly toys, pictures etc. may be used to lighten the topic.

'Sometimes, when I feel nervous about something, I get these big butterflies fluttering in my belly. Other times, I might feel a little sweaty, or a little sick. Other times, I might even need to pee really bad or feel my throat get a little tight. I wonder if anyone else here has experienced these feelings? What happened?'

The facilitator will allow the children and their parents to describe times where they felt anxious, why they were anxious and what happened. The facilitator will describe the symptoms of anxiety in a developmentally age-appropriate way and normalise these symptoms. They will then introduce the topic of this session and advise that helpful strategies will be taught today in a way that invites the children to participate further.

> ✓ Purpose of session today
>
> ✓ Thank participants for their attendance.

2. Naming my fears

Part of managing anxiety in children is naming their fears or stressors and making them concrete. Children under 10 may struggle to understand general terms, and rather may benefit from concrete external wording to separate the anxiety from them as a person (e.g. anxious about meeting new friends rather than socially anxious). However, for the purpose of this programme, parent and child will come up with a limited number of these fears during the session, but will be encouraged to work on others at home if needed.

> 'Let's start this session by thinking about something that makes us feel really nervous, something that gives us butterflies in our bellies. It might be something like walking down the stairs alone, or meeting new friends, or big noises. These things might make you "anxious". So, I'd like you to pick one, and then we'll talk about how we could make these butterflies go away with practice.'

ACTIVITY 1

The facilitator will split the large group into parent–child pairs and hand a small zip lock bag to each duo as well as a felt pen and a piece of paper. Each pair will then write the name of something that causes anxiety in the child (darkness, people, trains etc.) with the felt pen and lock the paper in the zip bag.

During this activity, the symbolism of separating the object of the children's anxiety from them should be emphasised, as should the locking of the zip lock bag. Children should be offered a sense of safety and control as they discuss their chosen worry. For some children, the notion that worries cannot hurt them may be tricky. Once each child has their 'anxious' item locked in the bag and feels safe and in control, the facilitator will then address the whole group again and introduce some strategies to address anxiety in children.

RESOURCES NEEDED

- A small zip lock bag

- A piece of paper.

✓ Thank children and parents for participating

✓ 'Locking up my fear' activity.

DISCUSSION

Is it possible that what makes us worried can be 'fixed' or 'helped'?

How do you think that would work?

Has anyone got a story of something that used to worry them, but doesn't anymore?

What happened?

3. 'I can make my worries go to sleep!'

In this section, the facilitator will emphasise to participants that whilst it is normal to have fears and worries, there are things they can do to make them 'go to sleep'. Simple exercises and activities will be presented and parents will be actively encouraged to participate and practise these with their children.

'Let me tell you something amazing today, children… I know something very special that I know will make you very happy. Did you know that we can make our worries go away? There are great games and activities we can play that will help. Who would like to learn about these magic tricks?'

Due to the age of the participants, worksheets are not recommended; however, a summary of strategies has been prepared at the end of this module (Worksheet 1) and should be provided to parents/carers for home practice. During the session, role modelling and role plays will be used instead.

DEEP BREATHS AND RELAXING OUR BODIES

The facilitator will start this section by running a small relaxation exercise. Parents may be invited to sit behind their children so their children are leaning back against them. This should make the children feel safe and allow the parents to role model with their own breathing and relaxation.

'The first magic trick we're going to learn today is called "relaxation" and is about deep breathing and making our bodies feel all nice and fuzzy. So why don't we start by taking three, nice, deep breaths?'

The facilitator will count to three as he or she inhales, and three as he or she exhales. Parents should be encouraged to mirror the facilitator with taking deep breaths. Then, the adults will be invited to assist the children in relaxing their bodies as they're taking deep breaths (shoulders, arms, neck etc.).

'How does this feel? Can you see how taking deep breaths and relaxing our muscles really help our bodies feel really good? This can be really helpful when we are worried. I hope you'll keep practising this one. Now, what about we learn a second magic trick?'

PRACTISING OUR HAPPY THOUGHTS

The facilitator will briefly remind the participants about bright and bubbly thoughts from module 4. Both parents and children will be invited to brainstorm some of the strategies taught in previous lessons and how they relate to anxiety management.

'Sometimes, we might get so worried about something that we start to think "dark and gloomy" thoughts. This happens to all of us, and that's normal, but what we know is that "bright and bubbly" thoughts make a big difference in how we deal with worries. So let's see who can remember what out bright and bubbly thoughts are, and whether we can make ourselves feel better about things we're worried about.'

LIMITED QUESTION TIME AND/OR WORRY TIME

The facilitator will briefly explain to the group that worrying for long periods of time only worsens feeling of anxiety. Parents in particular should be assisted with supporting their children with this. If need be, time at the end of the session could be used for parents-only discussion while the children are finishing their art.

'When we worry, we can "over-worry". That means think about our worries over and over again and this only makes it worse. So, one good exercise is to limit our worry-questions to three, or limit our time to be worried to 10 minutes a day. It's important to make sure that we don't let our worry brains take over too much, does that make sense?'

DISCUSSION

How does your body feel when it's worried? What do you notice about your heart, your belly? Your neck etc.? How did relaxing your body and taking deep breaths help? What would need to happen for you to try to worry less? Could you keep your worries to less than 10 minutes a day?

✓ Thank children and parents for participating

✓ 'Magic tricks' discussion

✓ Worksheet 1 for later – Summary of 'magic tricks'.

ACTIVITY 2: PUTTING IT ALL TOGETHER

The facilitator will then ask each parent–child team to form pairs and put both activities together: the zip lock bag and the magic tricks. Once in pairs, parents will assist their children in processing their 'worry' (locked in the bag) in the context of the strategies learnt today. Using deep breaths, muscle relaxation and bright and bubbly thoughts, parents (with the help of the facilitator) will assist children in practising these against the item they chose to lock up.

For example, they may discuss how taking deep breaths right before going to school as well as listing the positive things about school may help a child with some separation anxiety or worries about school etc. The facilitator will allow enough time for each pair to practise these at least once or twice before calling the group back together for the final activity of the day.

'What about we go back into pairs with our mum or dad now and see if we can practise our magic tricks with the worry that we've locked in the little bag? Let's practise our deep breaths, and our bright and bubbly thoughts and see what happens.'

DISCUSSION

How did the magic tricks work? What worked the best?
Something else that works is finding relaxing activities to do, like the ones we learnt in module 3. How would you like to try colouring a very special sheet called a Mandela? Lots of people find them very relaxing and we'll use this to end our session today.

Closing activity: 'Therapeutic colouring in'

The facilitator will invite the participants to practise relaxation strategies while undertaking a nice calming activity. The facilitator may choose to play some nice relaxing music in the background and ensure an appropriate atmosphere for this concluding activity. A couple of sample colouring sheets are included in this programme; however, similar materials are easily accessible online or through various books. Children should be allowed to self-regulate while colouring in with minimal disruptions from the adults, who will continue the discussion quietly separately.

RESOURCES NEEDED

- Colouring sheets (these are available through multiple channels but samples are available at the end of this module)

- Crayons/pencils/felt pens.

Closing down the session

The facilitator will summarise the module and activities with the participants. Anxiety is a common issue in children that they can learn to deal with better with lots of practice. The activities in this module should not be treated as one-off lessons to be learnt, but rather introductions to skills they can practise. Without ongoing and recurring practice, these strategies will not work and the facilitator should proactively advise parents of the nature of anxiety as well as the importance of practising the magic tricks as children engage with their colouring art.

'We've had a great time today, learning about our worries and some things we could do to make them go to sleep. Who, here, is going to try hard to practise our magic tricks? Let's try one more magic trick today and learn a special way to do art that will make our worries quiet. While you do this, mums and dads will have a little chat with me.'

CAN YOU FLY THROUGH YOUR WORRIES LIKE BREA THE BUTTERFLY?

SESSION 9: PARENTS' CORNER

'I CAN MAKE MY WORRIES GO TO SLEEP!'

Anxiety management issues generally run in families. They can be genetic, environmental or simply learnt behaviour. Consider your child's anxiety levels at the moment: are you surprised by them or were you expecting them due to family traits?

Today, we learnt about a few strategies. These are only some examples and/or foundation skills for your child to practise. It is important to keep reminding them and to keep improving on these as they grow up. However, if we consider that children learn from watching the adults around them, it is vital for you, your partner and other children to also be mindful of how you all manage your anxiety before expecting this younger child to manage their own issues. A few things to consider:

✓ How do you manage your own anxious feelings?

✓ What strategies could you teach your child or practise with them (yoga, swimming, reading, cooking, etc.)?

✓ Create a worry box with them. Allocate 10 minutes per day to it. Outside this time, make worries out of bounds for the whole family.

✓ Remember to practise all the bright and bubbly thoughts together (what worked well today, gratitude journal, things to look forward to, etc.).

WORKSHEET 1: Summary of 'magic tricks' for home practice

Today we talked about ways to make our worries go away. These work really well, but most of them will need practice at home, so to help with that, here is a list of magic tricks you can practise with Mum or Dad.

Deep breaths

Be brave and give it a go!

Happy thoughts

Talk to a grown up about your worries

Worry thoughts – max 10 minutes a day

Use your calm box

WORKSHEET 2: Colouring in art samples

|

Session | 10

Healthy Minds and Healthy Bodies

1. Welcoming participants

This module will be the last one of the programme. As an important session, it holds a double purpose: to teach the children about healthy bodies and to provide the opportunity for the children and their parents to debrief on the programme, evaluate it and facilitate closure. Some of the younger children may be reasonably adjusted to finishing the course. Others, particularly the older ones or those with attachment issues, may struggle with terminating the programme. It may have been a positive source of emotional debriefing and friendships forming, and facilitators should be mindful of the dynamics and individual children's adjustment. The facilitator will welcome the children and their carers back for their last session and gently remind them that it will be the last session of the programme. He or she may break the ice by inviting them to share examples of what they learnt and what they practised this week. When the participants have all had the opportunity to share their experience, the facilitator will introduce the topic of healthy bodies and healthy minds and assess the children's understanding of these.

> 'Good afternoon children and parents. Can you believe today is our last session? We've had such a great time! I hope you've learnt lots and will continue practising everything with your mum and dad after you leave here. Today, we're going to talk about our healthy bodies, and how having a healthy body can help us keep a healthy mind. Who here thinks they have a healthy body?'

✓ Housekeeping

✓ Success stories of the week

✓ Introducing the new topic of healthy bodies and minds.

---

2. What makes our bodies strong?

The facilitator will begin the session by introducing the topic of healthy bodies. To keep the children engaged in this different topic, he or she may invite the participants to show off their body endurance by doing small star jumps or little skips, and to watch each other's bodies as they move, breathe and react to exercise. Once the children are immersed in this week's topic, the facilitator will encourage them to list aspects of a strong and healthy body and make the link between nurturing their body and it working well. These may include:

- Solid bones

- Strong heart

- Fast muscles

- Good eyes and ears

- A belly to process food and vitamins

- Legs that run fast.

'I'd like you to look at your body, and pay attention to all the amazing things happening in it. How do you know whether your body is happy and healthy? What happens with it? Think of your bones, your muscles, your brain and so on.'

Having a strong and healthy body which works well enables you to do the things that keep your mind healthy, such as playing with friends, learning at school and spending time doing things you enjoy. Once children have made this link, the facilitator will invite them to form a group and settle for the next part of the session. The facilitator should then attempt to generate ideas from the children as to how they could nurture their bodies. Some examples may include:

- Drink milk/yoghurt/cheese for strong bones

- Eat healthy food like meat and vegetables

- Only have a small amount of 'treat' foods

- Exercise and play outside with our friends

- Limit electronic time to protect our brains and our eyes.

DISCUSSION

Look at our wonderful bodies. What do you think could keep them healthy or make them even healthier?

What do you think would happen if we ate bad food all the time? What about if we stayed in front of the TV too much?

Why does it matter what we eat, what we do and how we treat our bodies?

How do you think our brains and bodies work as a team?

ACTIVITY 1: 'THIS IS WHAT I CAN DO!'

The facilitator will invite children to pair up with their carer for this activity. Parent–child pairs will be split from the larger group and the worksheet on 'What it means to have a healthy body' (Worksheet 1) will be handed to each pair for more personal discussions. Through this process, parents, with the help of the facilitator, will assist children in learning about healthy eating, good exercises, important grooming as well as remind the children about how unique and wonderful they are (as per the teachings of module 1).

RESOURCES NEEDED

- Worksheet 1: 'What it means to have a healthy body'

- Crayons/pencils/felt pens.

The facilitator will conclude the session on healthy minds and bodies by getting the children and their parents to present the commitments they've chosen to make in the areas of healthy eating, exercise and grooming.

Closing down the session

The facilitator will then close the programme by summarising the teachings of the last 10 modules and inviting the children and their parents to continue working on their strengths and weaknesses. Using strength-based therapy tools, the facilitator will allow children to feel motivated, uplifted and proud of their growth and successes. Depending on the facilitator and/or the organisation hosting the programme's preference, an evaluation form should be handed out to all child–parent pairs, who may fill it in, anonymously if they wish, and return it to the facilitator. Finally, the facilitator will introduce the last activity to close the programme. This may take the form of a break-up party if appropriate. Evaluation forms for parents and children can be found as appendices at the end of this book. Additionally, it may be appropriate to have the parents/carers/teachers also fill out an evaluation as per the facilitator's discretion.

'This was our last lesson in this programme. It has been great getting to know all of you and to see your progress over the weeks. You need to remember how special you are and how you have learnt many skills you need to continue practising. I'm going to give you a form which will tell us what you liked or didn't like about this programme, and with Mum or Dad, you can fill it out. After this, we will do a final activity and receive our certificates.'

Closing activity: 'My happy new me!'

Once this has been done, the final activity for the programme will be offered (Worksheet 2: 'My happy new me!'). Whilst this worksheet is specifically about children's self-perception through craft, parents and facilitators will emphasise the children's growth at this time and assist them in putting this in the context of their future. They will brainstorm with the children the things that they enjoyed the most, the things they learnt and the things they will practise from this time forward.

Each child should build a warm and positive feeling as they're reminded of their strengths, potential and successes. Parents should also feel safe to terminate the programme, and referrals to appropriate ongoing services (if required) can be made at this point.

RESOURCES NEEDED

- Worksheet 2 printed on thick coloured paper
- Pencils/felt pens/glitter pens etc.
- Water paints if age-appropriate
- Craft material (foil, coloured papers, leaves, pasta, glitter glue etc.)
- Scissors if age-appropriate
- Glue.

INSTRUCTIONS

The facilitator will need to have prepared tables with material accessible to all participants. Water paints, pencils, felt pens, charcoal, chalk and other drawing material may be used and should have been prepared prior to the activity. As the children prepare for the activity, the facilitator will explain to them the purpose of it as well as the concept around growth. Children will be asked to draw their faces in a way that represents happy, healthy and growing little people.

Children will be encouraged to describe the benefits of the skills learnt and share them with the group. This should be organised in a positive and safe environment, ensuring that all children leave with a feeling of accomplishment. Facilitators should finally encourage them to continue practising the skills they have learnt and praise them for the change they have embraced.

TOMMY THE TIGER IS FIT AND HEALTHY, JUST LIKE YOU!

SESSION 10: PARENTS' CORNER

'WHEN I'M HEALTHY, I FEEL GREAT!'

Today marks the last session of the *Healthy Mindsets for Little Kids* programme for your child. It has been a privilege to get to know them and to watch you both develop a stronger bond.

For some of you, your children will have learnt skills they will be able to use. For others, there may still be a way to go to achieve the resilience you're after. Remember that when we work with children, we look at the whole family and not just the child, because in the family's dynamic we often find the reasons a child has developed one way or another (divorce or relationship status, discipline and parenting methods, communication skills, parents' own anger management, thinking patterns, grief and loss, amongst other things). *This is not a bad thing*, but a normal occurrence in every family. I would encourage all of you to look at your child in a family context and apply some of the strategies they have learnt to the whole family. As a final challenge, consider the following:

✓ How committed is the whole family to keeping up with the lessons taught through the programme?

✓ Consider resilience as a journey: what else could you implement and practise as you exit?

✓ What support is around you? Could you benefit from more? Do you know where to access it?

✓ Practice makes perfect. I hope you'll keep up the good work in the future!

✓

WORKSHEET 1: What it means to have a healthy body

Having a healthy body is important! Eating healthy food, exercising regularly and grooming ourselves are things that will make us feel good and fit. Let's talk about what those things mean for us.

HEALTHY EATING

Some foods are 'everyday' food and others are 'sometimes' food. We need to pay attention to what we're eating and how often. It is important to eat lots of fresh fruits and veggies and to love our bodies. It's not about our shape but about being healthy!

One thing I will try to improve with my healthy eating:

_____

_____

_____

_____

_____

HEALTHY EXERCISE

We need to exercise every day for our legs to grow and our muscles to stretch. It's easy, like jumping on the trampoline after school. It is important to exercise every day, but within limits. Too much can be a problem too!

One thing I will try to improve with my body exercises:

_____

_____

_____

_____

_____

PERSONAL GROOMING

Cleaning our teeth, brushing our hair and changing our underwear and socks are important too! And bonus points if we can do this without Mum or Dad telling us!

One thing I will try to improve with my personal grooming:

_____

_____

_____

_____

_____

WORKSHEET 2: My happy new me

|

APPENDICES

List of Appendices

✓ Programme Flyer

✓ *Healthy Mindsets for Little Kids* Application Form

✓ Welcome Letter to Parents

✓ Attendance Roll

✓ Attendance Certificate for Kids

✓ Feedback Form for Kids

✓ Feedback Form for Parents.

'HEALTHY MINDSETS FOR LITTLE KIDS'

✓

Healthy Mindsets for Little Kids is a resilience programme for children aged 5–9. The programme is run over ten weeks during the school terms/intensively over four days in the school holidays at (location)_____ on (dates) _____ from (time) _____,

The course is facilitated by (name) _____ with qualifications and experience in

_____

_____

_____.

The sessions will address:

+ Positive self-image

+ Communication skills

+ Assertiveness training and social skills

+ Positive thinking

+ Grief and loss

+ Healthy bodies and healthy minds

+ Anger and frustration management

+ Anxiety and stress management.

The cost is _____ per child for the whole programme and covers insurance, resources and admin costs. This particular programme is designed for children who have early symptoms of low resilience, anxiety, social difficulties or simply could benefit from universal and preventative interventions. To enquire about having *Healthy Mindsets for Little Kids* run in your local school, contact your school principal with a copy of this brochure.

Signature: _____

Business details:

✓

Application to join *Healthy Mindsets for Little Kids*

By filling out the application form, you agree that you have read the Additional Information attached.

Name of child: _____ Age: _____

School and Year level: _____ Phone number: _____

Address: _____

_____

Email or mobile number for notification: _____

Who referred you to this programme? _____

Reasons for wanting to join programme:

_____

_____

_____

_____

_____

_____

Relevant child and family history:

_____

_____

_____

_____

_____

_____

Signature: _____

ADDITIONAL INFORMATION

1. *Healthy Mindsets for Little Kids* is a resilience programme for children aged 5–9. The programme is run by (name) _____ on (days) _____.

2. (Name) _____ is a (profession) _____ with (qualifications and experience) _____ _____.

3. The purpose of the programme is to build resilience in children who are at risk of developing low self-esteem and depression, or attachment issues. It aims at improving confidence and assertiveness levels as well as general wellbeing.

4. Sessions are held at _____ on _____ from _____.

5. Participation cost is _____ per child per term upon acceptance of a place on the programme.

6. Due to the large demand for the programme and the small group number requirement, *ten* children will be accepted into each group on the programme. Each application will be evaluated and offers will be sent to the parent either via email or text message one week after the term's deadline.

7. Applications and referrals (if applicable) can be emailed to _____ or posted to _____ _____.

8. Children need to have the attention span to sustain 1.5 hours of discussion and activities as well as the social skills and willingness to interact with the other participants and facilitator. In the event of a child not able to cope behaviourally, their parents will be notified and the child's offer of a place on the programme may be withdrawn.

9. Referrals from teachers, GP or other professionals will be accepted and considered in the offers given.

10. Some of the topics discussed will be:

    • Healthy self-view

    • Positive thinking

    • Emotional regulation

    • Manners

    • Healthy relationships/friendships

✓

- Communication
- Anger management
- Anxiety management
- Healthy bodies.

We thank you for your interest and hope to work with your family in the future.

Yours in resilience,

_____

(Name and signature)

Healthy Mindsets for Little Kids Attendance Sheet

✓

NAME	Fees	Dates									

✓

Certificate of Attendance

Awarded to

_____

For successfully completing the
Healthy Mindsets for Little Kids resilience programme.

Modules include:

✓ Self-esteem

✓ Communication skills

✓ Anger and frustration management

✓ Grief and loss

✓ Positive thinking

✓ Healthy relationships

✓ Body image

Keep up the good work!

_____   _____

Facilitator   Date

Feedback Form for Kids

Dear Friend,

Thank you for participating in *Healthy Mindsets for Little Kids* this term. I have enjoyed our time together and hope that you have learnt a few skills you will use in the future.

Name (optional): _____

What was the best part of the programme? (A particular activity, a particular session or something you learnt?)

_____

_____

_____

_____

_____

_____

What did you enjoy the least in the programme? (A particular activity, a particular session or something that bored you?)

_____

_____

_____

_____

_____

_____

Circle how you feel about the programme:

✓

Do you have a message for the teacher (facilitator)?

_____

_____

_____

_____

_____

_____

_____

Do you have other comments?

_____

_____

_____

_____

_____

_____

Feedback Form for Parents

Dear Parents,

Thank you for enrolling your child in *Healthy Mindsets for Little Kids* this term. I have enjoyed my time with you both and hope that they have learnt skills they will use in the future.

I would really appreciate if you could take five minutes and fill in this form for me. It will help me provide a better programme for other children in the future. If appropriate, I'd love to hear how the programme helped your child and family down the track.

Name (optional): _____

As a parent, what feedback did you get from your child regarding the programme?

_____

_____

_____

_____

_____

Is there a particular session that was beneficial to you or your child?

_____

_____

_____

_____

_____

Is there a particular session that was not well received by your child? If so, why?

_____

_____

_____

_____

_____

✓

As a family and given your personal reasons for enrolling your child in the programme, have you noticed any changes in your child's behaviour?

_____

_____

_____

_____

_____

_____

How would you rate the facilitator and why?

_____

_____

_____

_____

_____

Overall how would you score your experience with the programme (on a scale of 1 to 10, 1 being bad and 10 being great). Circle the number:

| 1 | 2 | 3 | 4 | 5 | 6 | 7 | 8 | 9 | 10 |

Any other comments:

_____

_____

_____

_____

_____

_____

Kindest regards,

_____